Electric Pressure Cooker Guide and Cookbook

A Complete Guide to Get Started

Electric Pressure Cooker Guide and Cookbook

Table of Contents

Introduction

For most home cooks, the only problem that they face today is the lack of time. Cooking is a time consuming process considering that there are several foods that cook slowly and take several minutes to be done to perfection. However, with the introduction of pressure cooking, you can not only save time but also make your favorite dishes every single day.

Whether you are someone juggling between your home, kids and work or just a single person who has absolutely no time to wait for the food to cook, pressure cooking is the ideal choice for you. Instead of spending lots of money eating unhealthy food outside, making a small investment on a pressure cooker is highly recommended. You can try out several recipes, including the ones you really love and have them all ready in just a couple of minutes. Pressure cooking is so convenient that several experienced cooks and chefs are turning to it for some much needed assistance.

The electric pressure cooker, especially, is the most convenient kitchen gadget to have. Not only does it consume very little storage space, it is also extremely easy to clean. As for the cooking, the taste is just as good as your regular stove pressure cooker. Your electric pressure cooker does everything for you from adjusting the cooking time to keeping your dish warm after it is completely done.

Unlike the traditional cooker, where a good deal of time is consumed in bringing the cooker up to temperature before setting the timer and actually depressurizing it after your dish is done, the electric cooker is completely independent after you have pushed the start button. There is no need to babysit your electric pressure cooker. And what's best is that there is no fear of the cooker bursting, leaving your walls, cupboard and ceiling splattered with all the contents of your favorite food.

With an electric pressure cooker, all it takes is a bit of practice to understand how it works. Until you are sure, this book can take you through the exact process of making your electric cooker the handiest equipment that you have ever owned. There are several new types and models that are released regularly. Each one has several more programs that make it more convenient.

For a basic overview of an electric pressure cooker, read the following chapters. If you already have an electric pressure cooker and are comfortable using it, go straight to the recipes and enjoy!

Book Overview

This book takes you through the basics of using an electric pressure cooker. You can thoroughly understand how pressure cooking works. With this understanding, you will be able to use your electric pressure cooker to its best. You will also be able to experiment with new dishes when you understand the principle of pressure cooking. The book gives you a complete insight into the history of pressure cookers including its evolution over the last few decades.

You will also be able to learn about the different types of electric cookers that are available in the market. The basic differences and the additional programs available are also discussed in detail. This will help you understand what type of cooker you need to invest in depending upon the requirements of your family. You can also make the right choice based on the type of food that you eat on a regular basis. There are several factors like the amount of food, the frequency of use and also the type of cuisine that you are used to, that govern the type of electric cooker that you will purchase.

By the time you are through with this book, you will know exactly how to operate it as all the minute details like time conversions are discussed. For those of you who are not sure of what you can actually cook with an electric pressure cooker, this book gives you a list of 100 interesting recipes that you can try out. This includes ideas for breakfast, lunch, dinner, soups, snacks and dessert. You can enjoy all these healthy recipes with just a regular electric pressure cooker.

The basic aim of this book is to help all the readers make an informed decision when they purchase an electric pressure cooker. For those who already have an electric cooker that has been sitting in the attic in the same box that it came in, this is the complete handbook to make good use of your electric pressure cooker. Unlike a regular manual that only tells you the different programs and buttons available on your appliance, this book covers every single detail you need to know to use the electric pressure cooker correctly and safely.

Chapter 1: What is an Electric Pressure Cooker?

The History of Pressure Cooking

The first attempt to use steam to reduce the time taken to cook was made in the year 1679 by French Physicist Denis Papin. Papin invented a device known as the steam digester which worked on a principle similar to the pressure cooker that we use today. He devised an airtight cooker that worked by increasing the boiling point of water using steam. This resulted in faster cooking. Unfortunately, this benchmark in cooking technology was not considered a scientific study when he presented it to the Royal Society of London. It was only much later that he was accepted as the member of this society.

The earliest known pressure cookers were manufactured by George Sutbrod in Stuttgart in 1864. He made pressure cookers out of cast iron. Although there were so many initial designs and concepts presented with regard to pressure cooking, the first patent for pressure cooking was received in the year 1919. It was granted to Jose Alex Martinez by Spain. It was named 'olla express' which when translated means express cook pot.

Pressure cookers became available for home use only in 1938 when Alfred Vischler designed the Flex Seal Speed Cooker in New York City. Vischler presented this design as the first pressure cooker specifically designed for safe use at home. The pressure cooker received a lot of success which set European and American Manufacturers after it. The first pressure cooker manufactured for home use was unveiled at the New York World's Fair at 1939. It was presented by the National Presto Industries which was then known as the "National Pressure Cooker Company". This was the first company to manufacture its own pressure cookers.

Pressure Cookers and the World War

It was when America was about to enter the Second World that manufacturing of pressure cookers came to a standstill. During this period any facility that was meant for civilian use was converted to make way for war production. While cookers were not manufactured anymore, canners became more and more popular commercially. The GIs overseas began to demand for more commercial pressure canners during this time.

Things changed towards the 1940s when America made peace with Europe and the Pacific. This is when commercial production of the pressure cooker was like never before. There were almost eleven manufacturers that cropped up overnight. More than eighty five different kinds of pressure cookers or saucepans, as they were known back then became available. The prices of these cookers also fell drastically. Sadly, there were also many unscrupulous manufacturers who produced low quality products at low prices only because they wanted to capitalize on the demand. By then, consumers became aware of three specific benefits of the pressure cooker:

- Meals could be prepared in 1/3rd the time.
- The flavor and color of the food could be retained.
- The minerals and the vitamins in the food could be retained.

However, the production of low quality cookers led to some serious skepticism. By then, there were several horror stories of exploding cookers and related injuries. That is when the smaller companies began to drop out, making way for companies that were seriously involved in the development of
Better, safer and more foolproof units.

It was the pressure cooker that revolutionized cooking in an average home. After the Second World War, the popularity of the pressure cooker grew, no doubt, but the advances in cooking technology were so many that the cooker began to get overshadowed. People wanted more convenience than the pressure cooker could offer. It was only in the late 1960s and the early 1970s that people began to understand the health benefits associated with the pressure cooker.

Since then, there have been several variants of the pressure cookers. They were initially known as pressure canners as they were able to use the jars that were used in canning. Foods like pickles were preserved through the canning method. Today, there are special cookers that are designed especially for canning. The regular one is not recommended as there is a definite risk of botulism poisoning. This is because the amount of heat and pressure required to kill all the microorganisms is not provided by the regular pressure cooker. There are also special pressure cookers that have been designed to help sterilize hospital and laboratory equipment's. This equipment is known as an autoclave and is an essential part of hygiene in the health industry. There is also a special variant of the pressure cooker which is also known as the pressure fryer. The concept is the same but instead of steaming, food is actually fried under pressure. It is quite obvious that the pressure cooker cannot really be used for frying and hence, a new device especially for that was necessary.

Did you know that the food industry refers to the pressure cooker as a retort or a canning retort? Despite the several names and the several types of this equipment, the basic principle remains the same.

What exactly is canning?

During the Napoleonic wars, the process of canning was introduced. During these wars, malnutrition was a major concern. The French armed forces were being prepared for Napoleon's campaign against the Russians at that time. So, he had to make sure that the troops had better access to food. He decided to offer 12000 Francs to someone who could find a solution to store food well.

This solution came from Nicholas Appert who devised an ingenious method to store food. This method was known as "appertization". All the fresh foods were placed in a wide mouthed jar that was then heated in a water bath with boiling water. These jars were then sealed with corks.

The principle was quite simple. It worked on the same principle as wine which was stored in airtight bottles, preventing it from spoiling. Soon Appert actually started a vacuum packing plant. This was the earliest known application of canning. The design of the vacuum packing plant was improved by his nephew, leading to the canning industry that we know today.

This French military secret was leaked across the English Channel. Then, commercial canning factories were started in England in 1813. The effectiveness of canning was reinforced when Louis Pasteur proved that the growth of microorganisms was the cause of food spoilage.

Canners or Home Use

Pressure cookers were recommended for canning at home. The first pressure cooker that was available commercially was the huge industrial sized vessel. They were only used in commercial canneries. Then, the thirty gallon canner that was used in hotels and institutions was introduced. The size of the pressure cooker became smaller with the thirty gallon canner which was manufactured by National Presto. Following that, ten gallon models that were ideal for home use became available.

These models were made of lightweight aluminum. Canning was the most preferred method of storing food before the refrigerator came into being. The only obvious risk of canning was food poisoning which was brought to people's attention by the United States Department of

Agriculture. They recommended only foods that were low in acid to be stored through canning. Until refrigeration came into being, canning was the only known method of storing food.

The Predecessor of the Automatic Pressure Cooker

Automatic utensils were practically unheard of at the time when the pressure cooker was gaining popularity. It was the brilliant invention by Holcomb and Hoke that made way for automated cooking. In the year 1896, the company came up with an aluminum pressure cooker that was capable of self-regulation. They named it the "Thermo Chef" and the cooker came with a thermostat, a gas burner and the cooking utensil. The entire equipment was mounted on a stand with legs. The stand was actually bolted to the floor.

The only problem with this pressure cooker was its price. It was too expensive for the average American family at $76.85. Thousands of models of this novel cooking equipment were manufactured. None of them were sold as every family could afford domestic help at that time and, hence, did not require any self-regulating utensil. It is quite unimaginable to cook today without timers and automatic equipment, isn't it? But, it looks like the people of those times had entirely different beliefs. Maybe Holcomb and Hoke needed to study the purchasing habits before throwing this rather amazing utensil at a market that was not ready.

The point, however, is that this was the beginning of the electric and automated pressure cooker that is such a boon for modern cooks.

How an Electrical Pressure Cooker Work - The Technology

A few physics lessons are mandatory before you actually understand how a pressure cooker works. It is quite simple. We all know that water boils at 100∘C. After water reaches this temperature, no matter how long you continue to heat it, it remains at the same temperature. It only changes into steam which is also at the same temperature.

Now, the pressure cooker adopts a unique method where the temperature of the steam is actually increased. This is made possible only by putting it under pressure. When the vessel is covered with a certain amount of pressure, the steam is not allowed to escape. As a result, the temperature and the pressure inside the vessel continue to rise. The heat transfer potential of steam is also a lot higher than water which makes it the most preferred medium to cook food.

When you trap steam in a vessel and cover it with a tightly sealed lid and allow the pressure to build, the temperature rises accordingly. For instance, it you apply a pressure of about 15psi, the temperature of the steam rises to approximately 120∘C. As a result the food cooks a lot faster.

Now, the question that arises here is, how does the food remain undistorted despite the application of pressure? The answer is simple. The pressure applied on the surface of the food is uniform which prevents it from being distorted. Also, irrespective of the amount of food that is being cooked, the effective pressure from the surface to the center is the same.

Decoding the Pressure Cooker

The Parts

Every pressure cooker comes with some basic components that allow it to function as required. These parts include:

- THE PAN

The cooker comes with a metal body that is usually made of aluminum or stainless steel. This body comes with insulated handles on both sides that allow you to hold it with both hands.

- THE LID

The lid is the most important component for obvious reasons. The lid locks with a distinct click sound in the regular pressure cooker. It is lined by a rubber gasket that helps make it airtight allowing the steam to be trapped within. Always check that the gasket is properly in place. There is a pressure regulator on the lid that allows you to place a weight on it to maintain the pressure inside the pan. Sometimes, there is a pressure indicator that tells you how much pressure is being built inside the pan. There are safety devices that help release pressure safely when required

- OTHER ACCESSORIES

There are several other accessories like the steam basket, the trivet and the metal divider that come along with the pressure cooker.

Functioning

Steam is highly efficient in transferring heat to food and cooking it faster. The interesting property of steam is that it does not burn or damage the food that you are trying to cook.

Heat transfer is the basic principle that is applied in the pressure cooker. Take an oven and a tea pot to understand the difference. It is possible to put your hand inside an oven that has been heated to about 250∘C and not really burn your hand. But if you happen to place you hand over a tea pot that is boiling, your hand will scald immediately. This is because of the difference in heat transferring capacities of water and air. Air is a poor conductor of heat but moisture is a great conductor of heat. Think of it this way. If you are in water at 20∘C, it feels much colder than being outside at the same temperature. This is because the heat from your body is transferred to water faster than it is transferred to air.

In a pressure cooker where a considerable amount of pressure is applied on the water or other liquids inside it, the liquids do not actually boil. The reach a temperature that is higher than the boiling point enabling faster cooking. Even with the cooking time being cut down to almost $1/3^{rd}$, the nutritional value of the food is retained.

Once the lid of the pressure cooker is closed, a closed environment is created. This environment forces the steam through the food causing heat transfer. In a cooker, the pressure ranges from 10 to 15 psi. This allows the temperature to go up to almost 120∘C. The fiber present in the food becomes tender almost immediately. The flavors mingle well and the steam retains the nutrition and is condensed within the cooker, retaining the nutritional value of the food.

In an electric cooker, the heating element is the main component. This component allows a conversion of electricity into heat. When electricity passes through this heating component, a standard amount of resistance is experienced. This resistance leads to the production of heat. Besides the difference in the source of heat, the principle of pressure cooking remains the same with the electric cooker.

Chapter 2: Essential Benefits of the Electric Pressure Cooker

When you invest in a good electric pressure cooker, you can be assured that it is a long term investment. A good electric pressure cooker lasts for at least 10 years.

It is an extremely versatile and beneficial piece of equipment that is a great investment for a novice or an experienced cook. The essential benefits of an electric pressure cooker include.

A Healthy Lifestyle

For many people the primary reason for eating out is the lack of time to prepare a meal at home. But with the pressure cooker you can be in and out of the kitchen in no time and still make a wholesome meal for yourself and your entire family. Like it has been mentioned a couple of times before, your cooking time reduces to $1/3^{rd}$.

The time factor is important as it is the primary cause of erratic eating habits that lead to several health issues. When you are able to cook at home, you can avoid eating at fast food restaurants who pack their foods with salt, high fat and even preservatives and artificial flavors. With pressure cooking, the flavor of the food is retained a lot better than just boiling the food.

Another important thing is that the nutrients in the food are retained when pressure cooking is used. With an electric pressure cooker, the steam that is trapped in the vessel retains the nutrients. In case of boiling, the steam escapes, taking your nutrients out in air. When you pressure cook your food, the amount of oil used is practically nil.

Most of your food is steamed and even the naturally existing fat can be drained away when you do so. As a result, if you need to maintain a fat free diet, the pressure cooker is the ideal way to achieve this. In more ways than one, cooking with an electric pressure cooker is the most convenient and healthy cooking medium that you can use.

Eco Friendly Cooking

The electric cooker enables you to cook faster than you could cook in an oven or a microwave. The direct and most obvious effect of reduced cooking time is the reduction in fuel consumption. Research shows that you can bring down your fuel expenditure by almost 70% with an electric pressure cooker. You also get certified energy efficient electric cookers that are designed to save energy. Unlike the regular gas stove pressure cooker, the electrical cooker does not result in greenhouseemissions either. Hence, the electric pressure cooker is an ecologically friendly appliance.

Economical

First, you save a lot of money on fuel consumption. Since the electric pressure cooker takes very little time to cook your food, the units of electricity consumed are equally low making it the ideal choice.

You save almost 8 to 10 hours of cooking time each week which results in extremely high savings. The cooking speed of the electrical pressure cooker is incredible. For instance, a beef stew or even a simple bean soup that takes at least 45-60 minutes to cook completely, is ready in less than 15-20 minutes. As a result, you are able to reduce your cooking time and the energy consumption by 70%.

The result of this is that you have more resources to invest in better quality produce at the supermarket. You can also buy food in bulk and use the pressure cooker to cook large quantities of food in under an hour.

You can actually prepare for the main course for all the meals for one whole week with the help of the pressure cooker. Maybe that's why the pressure cooker is known as the original 'fast food' machine.

Indirectly, using an electric pressure cooker can save on cooling costs during warmer months. The electric pressure cooker does not heat up the kitchen like ordinary vessels. As a result, there is no wastage on cooling costs.

And finally, how can we forget the large diner bills? When you begin to cook at home, thanks to the convenience of the electric pressure cooker, you will also notice that the amount of money you spend on each meal is also considerably reduced.

So if you are looking for a cooking option that is easy on your pocket, you could consider investing in a good quality pressure cooker.

Safety and Dependability

The electric pressure cooker is a lot safer than the stovetop pressure cooker because depressurizing is automated with this appliance. All you need to do is program the appliance correctly. Following that, your electric pressure cooker will self-regulate everything. Unlike the stove cooker which comes with the risk of bursting or exploding, the electric pressure cooker is a lot safer. Of course, even with the regular cookers there are several models that have been introduced in the market with special safety features. The electric pressure cooker is especially user friendly and comes with several advanced features that are designed to make it 100% safe.

If you have to prepare a meal for guests who arrive suddenly or if you have been too delayed at work, all you need to do is throw in the contents of your favorite dish and program the pressure cooker. Not only is the cooking time reduced, there is also no need to monitor the cooker till your dish is fully ready.

Extremely Versatile

You can use the electric pressure cooker to braise, steam, fry, sauté or even simply warm your food. You can cook absolutely anything with your electric pressure cooker. Whether it is grains and meat that take a considerably long time to cook or even a bunch of carrots, the pressure cooker is the perfect utensil.

There are also several accessories that come along with the electric pressure cooker that can double as saucepans and even serving vessels. You don't need an oven either when you invest in a good electric pressure cooker. You will have settings that let you even bake a cake. You can altogether replace the microwave with the electric pressure cooker as the latter performs all the tasks faster and more efficiently.

In conclusion, investing in an electric pressure cooker is a great idea. The portability of this appliance also helps you cook on the go. If you are planning a camping trip, all you need is a portable power generator to cook any dish you want. With the kind of lifestyles that people lead today, the electric pressure cooker is definitely a boon. Besides, there are several small benefits like having more time to spend with your family that can actually have great implications in your life. So, even at a philosophical and a psychological level, the electric pressure cooker comes across as an excellent investment.

Chapter 3: Types of Pressure Cookers

There are several models and makes of electric pressure cookers that are available to us. They can be differentiated on the basis of the material that they are made from, the type of programming options available and several other factors.

Broadly speaking, however, there are three types of pressure cookers that have been developed since the conception of the pressure cooker. They are segregated based on the features that are available. The three main types of pressure cookers are:

The First Generation Pressure Cookers

The pressure cookers that belonged to this generation are the ones that you would typically find in your grandmother's kitchen. The pressure cookers operate with the help of a weight modified valve. These valves usually make an inherent jiggling sound while the food is cooking as they tend to release pressure during the process of cooking food.

This pressure cooker functions on the same principle as the piston in a steam engine and can, hence, be extremely noisy. This old style of pressure cooker usually comes with only one weight modification option. However, there are a few modern styles of the "old style cooker" that come with the option to change the pressure level with the help of different weight valves.

Several modern pressure cookers that are priced lower are modifications of the first generation cooker. They come with several additional safety features and also technical improvements that help them perform better.

Second Generation Pressure Cooker

These cookers are also known as "new generation cookers" or "latest generation cookers". They function rather differently from the first generation cooker. The valve is spring loaded and is usually not visible. This generation of pressure cooker also comes with two pressure settings. The most important feature of the second generation pressure cooker is that there is no need to release the steam while the cooker is operational. For this reason, they may sometimes be referred to as "non venting" cookers. The only time the pressure is released is when the cooker is opened.

To make sure that it is completely safe to use, this type of pressure cooker comes with a feature that lowers the temperature automatically. There are some second generation pressure cookers that allow the operator to manually release the pressure using a dial which adjusts the spring to release the pressure and the steam.

The Third Generation Pressure Cooker

The Electric pressure cooker is also known as the third generation pressure cooker. This type of pressure cooker comes with a heating source that is electronically regulated. The operating pressure is maintained by this heating source. These cookers also come with a spring loaded valve like the second generation cooker.

Apart from two more pressure settings, this type of pressure cooker comes with a timer and settings that can keep food warm after cooking. One main difference is that this type of cooker does not allow cold water pressure release.

You must be very careful when you release the pressure with the electric pressure cooker. While some are self-regulated, there are a few that require you to release the steam with the help of the valve.

The electric pressure cooker itself has undergone several changes since its conception. Continue reading to get a though understanding of the types of electric pressure cookers that you can find in the market today.

Types of Electric Pressure Cookers

In the year 1991, the patent for an electric cooker was issued. During that time the concept of pressure cooking was already quite popular. There were several technological advancements like the invention of sensors that the developers of pressure cookers made use of.

First Generation Electric Pressure Cookers

The first generation of electric pressure cookers consisted of sensors that were able to monitor the temperature and pressure settings and control them as required. It came with several safety features that made it very user friendly.

The first and most important safety feature was the one that did not allow the user to open the lid until the temperature and pressure had reduced. According to recommended safety standards.

Second Generation Electric Pressure Cookers

The next generation of electric cookers were released somewhere around the mid-90s.These pressure cookers came with several additional programs like the automatic warming, delayed cooking and other presets. The safety features included an alarm that went off if a valve was open or if the lid was not closed properly. The cooker would simply shut itself off if there was no immediate response to this alarm.

The Third Generation Electric Pressure Cookers

The cookers that we see today are known as third generation electric cookers. These cookers come with a microprocessor which is like a tine CPU that is fitted into computers normally. Using this processor, it is possible to provide complex programs that are designed for different kinds of foods. The pressure and temperature will be automatically regulated as per the requirement of the food that the cooker has been programmed for.

Electric pressure cookers of all three generations are available. The common factor among the three generations is the convenience of use and operation. There are different materials that these cookers are made of. The most preferred type of electric cooker is the one with a nonstick interior and a heat proof exterior. There are different sizes available ranging from 4 quarts to 8 quarts. They all offer three levels of pressure management and a gauge that allows the user to monitor the pressure level.

The Electric pressure cooker is quite different from the regular pressure cookers in various ways. The obvious difference is the heat source but there are several other important details that can help you figure out which one you prefer more. There is a detailed list of differences between the two types of pressure cookers in the next chapter.

Chapter 4: The Difference between a Regular Pressure cooker and an Electric Pressure Cooker

Although the electric pressure cooker and the regular pressure cooker work on the same basic principle, there are some differences that change the way you operate the appliance. For instance, while the electric pressure cooker requires absolutely no monitoring to bring to the required pressure and temperature, the time taken to reach the desired value is longer. The difference in time is just a few minutes. However, pressure release with an electric cooker is almost double as the heat source cannot be removed. Additionally, the cooker is completely insulated resulting in longer time for heat loss. At the same time, the ability of the pressure cooker to maintain the heat within its coil makes it 60% more efficient in electricity consumption. There are several such features of the electric pressure cooker and the stove top pressure cooker that can be compared in more detail. Below is a list of features for you to understand and make the right choice while purchasing a pressure cooker.

Comparison between the stove top and electric pressure cooker

STOVE TOP PRESSURE COOKER	ELECTRIC PRESSURE COOKER
Pressure Settings	
With the stove top pressure cooker, you have the option of multiple pressure settings. The maximum pressure that you can achieve with a stove top pressure cooker is 13-15 PSI while the lowest pressure you can achieve is between 6-8 PSI. Most recipes that you will find in cook books provide the timings according to these regular pressure settings. You can use a simple dial to shift between different pressure settings available with a particular model of the	With electric pressure cookers, the maximum and minimum pressure settings are quite different with each model. There are some models that can only provide pressure settings up to 6 PSI. However, there are others that can provide pressure settings ranging from 8 PSI to 13 PSI. Although some claim to be able to reach, 15 PSI, they only reach about 13. If your pressure cooker is unable to reach the desired standard of about 13 PSI, you will have to

pressure cooker. Usually the marking in the beginning are the low pressure mark while the one at the end is the high pressure mark.

provide additional cooking time as recommended in cook books. Most electric cookers come with a single pressure setting and some go up to a maximum of 2 pressure settings. In models that have two pressure settings, the higher setting is usually meant for cooking meat while the lower setting is to cook rice.

HEAT REGULATION

It is necessary to adjust the heat settings in the pressure cooker before you are able to obtain the required amount of pressure. For this, you must first heat the appliance at maximum heat and then reduce it to medium or low flame. With a stove top pressure cooker, a little bit of trial and error that is necessary to get the heat setting right for different kinds of foods.

With the electric pressure cooker, there is no need to monitor the heat regulation. This is because all the settings on an electric pressure cooker are pre- programmed. All you have to do is choose the recommended program for the type of food that you want to cook and press the start button

PRESSURE RELEASE

With the stove top pressure cooker, there are three types of pressure release options.
• Cold Water Release- It takes about 30 seconds to release pressure
• Normal Release- It takes about 2 minutes to release pressure
• Natural Release- It takes about 10 minutes to release pressure.
There may be additional pressure release features depending upon the model of the pressure cooker that you are using. There are certain guidelines for different pressure release modes. For instance, if you are cooking foods like legumes that foam while they are cooking, you must not opt for normal release through the main valve. For such foods, only cold release or natural pressure release is recommended.

In an electric pressure cooker, cold water release is not an option. There are two pressure release methods that can be used. This includes:
• Normal Release- 3 minutes
• Natural Release- 25 minutes

Even with the electric pressure cooker, it is recommended that you open the cooker using the Natural Release method for foods like legumes that foam while they are cooking

TIME TO DEVELOP REQUIRED PRESSURE

It takes about 11 minutes for a regular pressure cooker to come to the desired pressure level. This is also dependent on the type of heat source available and the capacity of the pressure cooker.

Usually, an electric pressure cooker takes about 14 minutes to reach the desired pressure level. This time varies as per the electric heat coil in the cooker and also the wattage of the electric cooker that you are using.

COOKING FEATURES AND SCHEDULER PROGRAMS

Except for a few German models, most stove top pressure cookers are not integrated with a timer. Therefore, you need to either watch a clock or set a separate timer to monitor the cooking time.

With stove topped cookers, there are no programs or scheduling features, usually. If the stove toped pressure cooker is used with an induction stove, it is possible to automate the timer on the system.

The Electric Cooker is the third generation pressure cooker which comes with a host of features. All electric pressure cookers consist of an integrated pressure cooker to monitor the time taken for certain foods to cook. As soon as the pressure cooker reaches the designated pressure value, it begins to countdown the timer automatically.

With recently introduced models, you also have several smart cook features that work with a thermostat and a pressure sensor. The programming and scheduling can be done as per the food that you want to cook. If you want to cook grains, for instance, there are some programs that allow you to soak the grains before cooking. You also have the delayed start feature with many models that allow you to delay the starting time by almost 12 hours.

SAFETY

Every stove top pressure cooker comes with a

There is a lid closure detection sensor that

lid that locks firmly in place. This ensures that the lid does not open when the pressure is being built. There is a primary over pressure valve to release any additional pressure that builds incase the heat source is not turned on. In case this primary release valve fails, there is a secondary pressure valve that will release the excess pressure. There is also an additional option of the emergency gasket where the gasket can be buckled and released though a cut in the lip of the lid. There are many more safety features depending upon the manufacturer of the pressure cooker.	ensures that the pressure cooker is closed securely. This is a mechanical system that remains functional even when the cooker is unplugged. The electric pressure cooker also comes with an over pressure release valve that ensures that any excess pressure that might be formed is released immediately. This valve gets activated in case the cooker is unable to turn off its heat source or reduce the heat as required. The emergency gasket pressure release allows the additional pressure between the lower pot and the inner pot of the cooker body to escape by buckling the gasket. The sensors in the cooker also make a note of the right pressure required to make sure that the food does not burn. If there is any extreme temperature or power fluctuation, the cooker is automatically disconnected with the help of the power protection sensor.
MULTIPLE USES	
With the stove top cooker, it is possible to use it as different utensils. For instance, without the lid, the pot acts as a saucepan.	The electric pressure cannot be used as a regular utensil. Only with some new models, you have the option to sauté some vegetables. You can also bake and brown the food with electric cookers that come with special cooking programs.
STORAGE	
Storing the stove top pressure cooker is easy as it fits in with your pots and pans.	For those using an electric cooker, it is necessary to allot some space on the counter. Electric cookers are usually bulky and are a little difficult to store.
HEAT SOURCE	
The heat source is external. It can be in the	The heating coil is integrated in the body of the

form of heat from a gas, electric, ceramic, induction or halogen gas stove. It can also be used over barbeques and campfires.	electric pressure source. This coil is heated electrically and responds to a thermostat that helps regulate the temperature.
MATERIALS USED AND DURABILITY	
Usually the body of this type of cooker is made using aluminum or steel. Stainless steel cookers are the most preferred ones as they are extremely durable. They are not damaged easily and can last as long as 20 years. It is only the gasket and the parts made of silicon that are subject to wear and tear. These parts can be replaced easily.	The electric cooker consists of a casing on the exterior which is made of thermal resistant plastic. The interior consists of a nonstick coating usually, although it may be entirely made of aluminum sometimes. It is very important to keep sharp objects away from the electric cooker as it is really easy to scratch the inner coating. There are new models that are made of durable stainless steel. The electronic system varies according to the model. There are some poor quality models that can experience electronic failures in just three years of continuous use.

While time matters to some people, durability is important to others. Some of you might want to invest in a cooker that will help you save some money while others may just want a multipurpose utensil that is easy to store. Depending upon what your need is, an electric pressure cooker or an on stove pressure cooker might be suitable. If you cannot make up your mind, just pick of one of each.

Chapter 5: Types of Pressure Release

When you are using a pressure cooker, one of the most important safety measure is the pressure release mechanism. If you are unaware of the methods of pressure release, it is quite possible that you might make way for unwarranted accidents in your kitchen. In addition to that, knowing the right pressure release method will also help you save time when you are really in a hurry.

Cold Water Quick Release:

This is the fastest way of pressure release. With an electric pressure cooker, you will get a quick release option. In the traditional cooker, in order to quick release the pressure, you must pour cold water along the edges of the cooker and slowly vent the steam as you do so. Only when all the pressure has been released is the cooker safe to open.

Unless your EPC has a quick release option, do not try the traditional method with it. Quick release is only suitable for food that can cook very fast.

Manual Release:

In most electric cookers, a manual release button or valve will be present. This method is usually used when one needs to add more ingredients or food into the cooker by interrupting the cooking of the contents that are already in the cooker. In case you are making meat, for instance, you would probably add the meat in first as it takes the longest time to cook. In case you want to add vegetables or spices to the meat that is cooking, you can opt for the normal release method.

Normal release is also a fast pressure release method but is not as fast as the cold water release method.

The Natural Release Method

This is a pressure release method which does not require any action to lower the pressure inside the cooker. All you have to do is turn the heat off and let the pressure drop slowly. This should take about 15 minutes. It is the most suitable method for foods that consume time to cook. Legumes and red meat cook best when the natural pressure release method is employed.

Now that you know of all the pressure release methods, you might want to check your electric pressure cooker for the options available. If any of the above options is missing, it means that you cooker has not been designed for it and that you must not try it!

Chapter 6: Translating Cooking Timings

Like we mentioned before, the time taken to cook with a stove top pressure cooker is quite different from an electric pressure cooker. All the cook books that you refer to regularly assume a certain pressure standard and base their timings on it. However, the electric pressure cooker does not reach the same pressure levels as the regular cooker. This means that there are a few alterations that you will have to make in the cooking method to get the same results with your electric pressure cooker.

Converting a Stove Top Pressure Cooker Recipe to an Electric Pressure Cooker Recipe

There are four steps that you need to take to get your cooking technique right with an electric pressure cooker:

1.   The liquid volume must be reduced: With any type of pressure cooker, a liquid is necessary to heat and create the right amount of pressure. With the stove top cooker, an external weight is usually applied on the steam vent. When the vessel reaches the required pressure level, the weight moves and releases the excess pressure to maintain the pressure levels. This means that the liquid that is released in the form of steam is lost. About ¾ of the water that you use is lost. In case of an electric pressure cooker, the loss of liquid is very less. So the amount of liquid that you use in an electric pressure cooker is 40% lesser than the stove top pressure cooker.

2.   Cooking time needs to be altered: The operating pressure is different for an electric pressure cooker and a stove top pressure cooker. Usually, a stove top pressure cooker works at about 15 PSI. It is a lot lesser for an electric pressure cooker. The standard pressure is 15PSI and say the difference in pressure between the standard and your electric pressure cooker is x, then you have to increase the pressure by x%. For instance, if the pressure in the electric cooker is 12 PSI, the difference is 3 PSI. So you have to increase the pressure by (3/15)*100 which is 20%. So if the average time taken to cook a certain dish is 10 minutes in the stove top pressure cooker, you will have to increase it by 2 minutes for the electric cooker.

3.   Time Taken to Heat should be changed: The time taken to heat the vessel to reach its optimum pressure is a lot higher for a stove top pressure cooker. Although the difference in heating time is not much, it is necessary to pay attention to this small detail.

4.   Pressure Release time is different: Even after the heat source is turned off, the food continues to cook as the pressure dissipates from the vessel. Since some recipes require you quick release to be done to perfection, it is quite important to understand the methods of pressure release and also the tine taken to release pressure in your electric cooker.

Cooking is not really rocket science. At least, that is not what it is meant to be. So when you are making time conversions or following recipe books, be prepared for some dish-mishaps. You may overcook or undercook your food. But with practice, there will come a time when you will definitely get it right.

As you continue to pressure cook your food, it will become a habit. You will instinctively know how much liquid is required or how much cooking time is required. For those who are just starting off, here is a chart with suggested cooking times. Of course, depending on the model of your appliance and other factors like the amount of liquid you put in, the cooking time will vary.

Cooking Schedule for your Electric Cooker

FOOD	TIME TAKEN (MINUTES)
FRUITS AND VEGETABLES	
Apple chunks	2
Whole Artichokes	8 to 10
Whole Asparagus	1 to 2
Fresh Beans, Whole or pieces	2 to 3
Shelled Lima Beans	2 to 3
Sliced Beets	3 to 4
Peeled Whole Beets	12 to 14
Florets and Spears of Broccoli	2 to 3
Brussels Sprouts	3 to 4
Quartered Cabbage	3 to 4
Cauliflower Florets	2 to 3
Corn on the Cob	3 to 4
Shelled Peas	1
Potato pieces	5 to 7

Whole potatoes	10 to 12
Small Potatoes	5 to 7
Fresh Spinach	2 to 3
Sliced Squash	1 to 2
Sweet Potatoes	4 to 5
Sliced Turnips	2 to 3
MEAT	
Roast Meat (Pork, Lamb, Beef)	40 to 60
Meat Cubes	15 to 20
Chicken Pieces	10 to 12
Whole Chicken	15 to 20
Stock	30
MISCELLANEOUS	
Barley	15 to 20
White Rice	5 to 7
Quinoa	7
Brown Rice	15 to 20

It is important to note that the settings and the timings might differ with different models of the Electric Pressure cooker. There are three possibilities with getting your cooking time wrong:

- The food is undercooked: If this happens, all you need to do is extend the timer of the electric pressure cooker and close the lid to let the food cook some more.
- The food is burnt: This is only possible if the amount of water you have put in the cooker is not adequate. The steam created within the cooker ensures that the food does not burn.
- The food is overcooked: If this happens, just remember to reduce the cooking time in future. There is nothing more you can do to fix this!

Handy Tips to Cook with an Electric Pressure Cooker

Cooking meat with an electric pressure cooker can be quite a challenge considering that there are several cuts of meat available for us to choose from. Here are a few tips that will help you cook the meat of your choice to perfection.

- Before you season the meat with salt and pepper, make sure you pat it dry completely.
- Unless mentioned otherwise, always sear the meat until it is slightly brown to bring out the best flavors.
- It is recommended that you use cheaper cuts and tougher meat in a pressure cooker. Since the meat is cooked under pressure, the fibers break down leaving the meat nice and soft.
- Before you carve whole poultry or even roast meat, allow the contents to first sit for about 15 minutes.
- All roast slices should be made against the grain of the meat.

Chapter 7: Choosing the Right Pressure Cooker

With electric pressure cookers, there are so many different types and models that it can get quite confusing for a first time shopper. However, knowing what to look for can really help you make the right choice in cookware for your kitchen.

There are a couple of simple things that will help you decide which electric cooker you want to buy:

Size

With electric pressure cookers, size definitely matters. There is a range of sizes that the electric pressure cooker is available in. Starting with cookers that are smaller than 4 quarts in size and there are a few that can go up to 10 quarts. The choice of size basically depends on the food that you cook and the number of people you usually cook for. If you typically eat foods like soups and stew, a large pressure cooker is ideal to cook for a large group or to cook a big batch to freeze and store. If you are cooking for a family of four, a 6 quarts cooker is ideal. You will also get larger sizes with come with additional accessories like streamer inserts.

It is always recommended that you buy a cooker that is slightly larger than the size that you think you will require. Most often people end up increasing the quantity of the food that they cook as they become familiar with the usage of an electric pressure cooker. Another advantage with larger cookers is that you can easily cook bulkier food items.

The real capacity of your cooker is only two thirds of the full capacity. This is because most foods expand as they cook. You can also expect a certain extent of foaming with some foods. So if you have a 4 quart electric pressure cooker, it is impossible for you to make 4 quarts of soup.

Material and Construction

The material that your cooker is made from is also an important factor in deciding of the cooker is right for you. Some cookers are made from aluminum. Aluminum is extremely light but it is not as durable as the stainless steel cooker. If you want an electric cooker that has a very thick base, you can also choose one that is lined with aluminum or copper. These metals help conduct heat and also retain the heat. The handles are also very important. The large the size of your cooker, the sturdier and larger should the handles be. It must definitely have a lid that locks in place to ensure complete safety while cooking. Although this is a standard feature, make sure you check it once before you make the purchase.

Instructions and Programs

With an electric pressure cooker, you can expect several programs that are meant to cook different kinds of food. The controls should be easy to read. The most important feature that an electric cooker should have is time adjustment to cook delicate foods. There must also be a heat diffuser at the bottom to make sure that the heat source does not scorch after repeated use. Some cookers come with a detachable pressure regulator. This is quite a useful feature as it allows you to control the cooker and the pressure settings better.

Miscellaneous

It is important for your pressure cooker to have multiple pressure settings. This makes it easier for you to cook different types of foods. The cooker should at least have one high pressure setting and one low pressure setting. This helps you cook tougher fibers like beef and also tender fruits and vegetables respectively.

It is important to check the pressure valve. Usually, an electric pressure cooker has a normal pressure release valve. If there is a quick release option, it can be quite beneficial as some recipes demand fast pressure release. The cold water method is, of course, not an option with the electric pressure cooker.

You must also check for parts that are easy to detach to make maintenance and cleaning easier. If your pressure cooker has too many dials and knobs, you cannot help but have food particles stuck in the nooks and crannies. It is difficult to clean and can become visually unpleasant over time.

The electric pressure cooker that you choose will be around for at least 10- 15 years. So, the only advice that is really relevant is, choose wisely!

Chapter 8: Cooking with the EPC: 100 Scrumptious Recipes

If you are a beginner, you are going to love this bit of the book. You will be amazed at the wonderful things that you can actually cook with your electric pressure cooker. These recipes are based on standard pressure settings and can be altered as shown in the previous chapters.

To make it easier for you to understand how to cook different kinds of foods, these recipes have been segregated as per the main ingredient used. The basic ingredients including various proteins like beef and chicken and the most commonly use vegetables have been discussed in detail in the following pages.

It was a pleasure to choose some of the best and easiest recipes for you. Hopefully, you have a blast preparing them for you and the rest of your family.

These recipes were cooked in a Wolfgang Puck Pressure Cooker that has only 3 options.

Heat, Cook and Warm. I used the Heat mode to sauté and brown, and when everything was ready to cook I just set the timer to the required time. If you have a different model you can

Experiment with the different cooking modes. It should be very easy!

And another tip…

I have been experimenting with different recipes and ways to use my pressure cooker and I have found one method that is quick, easy, and fun and the results are delicious. Its PRESSURE COOKING WRAPPED IN FOIL. You can make packets of all in one meals very fast and easy. The best results are with chicken breasts preferably boneless, skinless and split. I personally us individually wrapped, all natural chicken breast made by Natures Promise (Purdue has a similar product) that are about 6 oz. each. You can use any brand that you like but make sure they are not more then 1- 1 ½" inches thickif they are you can pound them with a meat mallet to flatten. You can let your imagination run wild here with the different ingredients that you use in these packets. Basically what you do is lay out a few sheets of aluminum foil on the counter (approximately 12" x 12") place the chicken breast on the foil and brush with olive oil on both sides and sprinkle with salt and pepper and any other spice that you like. Here is where you can get creative – brush on any type of sauce, (BBQ sauce is a good one) salad dressing (Italian is a good one) just use your imagination. Then pick your favorite vegetables and chop them up good. Pile the veggies on top of the breast or breasts and fold the foil to make a sealed packet, (not to tight). You can then put a rack or a trivet in the cooker or not, and add 1 ½ cups of water. Now place the packets on the rack or trivet or directly in the water with the seam side up.

Set the timer for between 8-10 minutes, that depends on your cooker and the thickness of the meat. I use a Wolfgang Puck 6 Qt Pressure cooker and I set the timer for 8 minutes. After the cooking time is up I release the pressure manually (pressure release knob) remove the packet or packets, transfer to a plate, let cool for a few minutes, open the packet and either eat directly from the packet or tip it on a plate and eat it. The chicken is juicy and the vegetables are well cooked. The best part is it that there is no mess and your meal is healthy and almost completely nonfat.

You can also do the same thing with fish filets. **You may need to experiment a little to get the timing right or your individual pressure cooker** and to see which sauces and veggies you like the best. My favorites are onions, mushrooms, spinach and tomatoes. I will include some of these recipes in the last part of the recipe section for you to try.

HAPPY COOKING!

SALADS FOR THE HEALTH FREAKS

Every meal should begin with a salad or should at least have a side of a healthy salad. With your electric pressure cooker at work, you won't have to eat boring raw salads with the same old dressing every day. Here are some interesting salads that you can try and experiment with.

Fresh Quinoa and Bean Salad

Ingredients

- Rinsed Quinoa seeds- ½ cup
- Black beans- ½ cup
- Diced Tomatoes- 1 cup
- Sliced or Diced Mini Cucumbers- 4
- Red Hot Pepper, diced- 1
- Cooked Corn- 1 can

For the Dressing:

- Oil – ½ cup
- Lemon Juice- ½ cup
- Cumin- 1 teaspoon
- Parsley- As per your preference
- Mint- few leaves
- Salt and pepper

Procedure

- Place the quinoa seeds in the cooker with 1 cup of water. Lock the lid and allow it to cook for 2 minutes.
- Release pressure manually when done, fluff up and remove to bowl...
- Place the black beans in the cooker with 3 cups of water. Close the lid, lock it into place, close the vent and set timer for 20 minutes.
- When time is up, allow pressure to reduce instantly, open the lid and remove.
- In a large salad bowl, mix the rest of the ingredients together. You can even add a little salt and pepper seasoning if you like.
- Add the baked beans and the cooked quinoa to this mixture.
- In a blender, process all the ingredients for the dressing. The dressing will acquire a creamy consistency when it is ready.
- Just toss the salad with the dressing and it is ready to be served.

Garden Salad with Boiled Peanuts

<u>Ingredients</u>

- Raw Peanuts in shell- 1 pound
- Bay Leay-1
- Chopped Tomatoes- 2
- Green pepper, diced- ½ cup
- Diced Sweet Onion- ½ cup
- Diced hot peppers- ¼ cup
- Diced celery- ¼ cup
- Fresh Lemon Juice- 2 Tablespoons
- Olive oil- 2 tablespoons
- Salt to taste
- Freshly Ground Black Pepper- ¼ teaspoon

<u>Procedure:</u>

- Take the skin off the peanuts and discard. Place peanuts in the pressure cooker.
- Close the lid, lock it into place, close the vent and set timer for 10 minutes.
- When time is up, allow pressure to reduce naturally
- When pressure is reduced, open the lid and remove the peanuts from the water.
- In a large bowl, mix the peanuts and the diced vegetables well.

Dress with lemon juice, oil, salt and pepper and your summer salad is ready to serve.

Sweet 'n' Spicy BBQ chicken salad

<u>Ingredients</u>

- Chicken Breasts(frozen) 1 Pound
- Water- 1/3 Cup

<u>For the sauce</u>

- Ketchup- ½ Cup
- Barbeque Seasoning- ¾ Spoon
- Red Pepper Flakes- As per your Taste
- Honey- 2 Teaspoons

<u>For Salad</u>

- Lettuce
- Spinach
- Tomatoes
- Pine nuts
- Walnuts
- Flax Seeds
- Cheese of your choice
- Dressing of your choice (I recommend thousand Island dressing)

<u>Procedure</u>

- Add the water to the pressure cooker.
- Place the frozen chicken in the pot with the water and close the lid.
- Set timer for10 minutes.
- In the meanwhile, separate your salad fixings in two different bowls.
- In a small bowl, mix all the barbeque sauce ingredients together. Adjust the sauce as per your taste.

- Once your cooker beeps, opt for the quick pressure release.
- Slice the chicken breasts into ½ inch strips keeping the chicken in the pot. The chicken will be raw in the middle but it will still be easy to cut.
- Pour your BBQ sauce over the chicken. The dish may look too watery but that is quite normal.
- Use the sauté or heat option and time your cooker for about 10 minutes. Allow the sauce to come to boil, after about 5 minutes to turn the chicken over and continue to cook it.
- You need to monitor this dish a little to make sure that the sauce does not become too thick. In the last five minutes, you need to stir the chicken well to ensure that the sauce sticks to all the pieces.
- When most of the sauce is stuck to the chicken, take the pieces out on a serving tray and turn your pot off.
- Lay the chicken on top of the salad and add a dash of seasoning over it before you serve.

Tip: When you turn the cooker off after removing the chicken pieces, pour 2-3 cups of water into the pot. This ensures that the sauce does not stick to the pan and burn.

SOUPS

There is nothing more satisfying than a big bowl of good soup. With an electric pressure cooker, making soups is a cake walk. No matter how many people you have over for dinner or lunch, you can make a rich, nutritious and filling soup and serve it to them. Add a side of bread and you will pass off as a great host. All you need is all the necessary ingredients and an electric pressure cooker that is big enough.

If you have a family recipe that you love, you can just make a few changes in the cooking method. You will see how much more time you can save by pressure cooking your soups. The best part is that all the nutrients in the vegetables and the meat that you use in your soup will be retained. So the healthiest and the easiest meal option is some soup or chowder.

Here is a list of my favorite soups that go perfectly with any food mood that I may be in. Of course, you can try out many more recipes as per your preferences

Traditional Jamaican Hot Soup

<u>Ingredients</u>
- Diced Bacon-
- Chicken Breast or beef chuck- 1 pound
- Shrimp- ½ pound
- Beef Broth- 1 can
- Water- 2 Cups
- Onion- 1 large
- Spinach- 1 pkg
- Thyme- 1/2 teaspoon
- Red or Green Pepper- 1
- Sliced Tomatoes- 1 can
- Bay Leaf- 1
- Salt to taste
- Pepper for seasoning
- Hot Sauce to taste
- Frozen Okra- 1 pkg
- Butter- 3 tablespoons
- Heavy cream- ½ cup
- Paprika to taste

<u>Procedure</u>
- Place the water, onion, bacon, chicken, and onion and beef broth in the pressure cooker. Then add the spinach, thyme, pepper, bay leaf, tomato, salt, pepper and hot sauce.
- In a separate pan, sauté the okra in butter over the lowest heat for about 5 minutes. Add it to the soup. (optional)
- Close the lid, lock it into place, close the vent and set timer for 10 minutes.
- When time is up, allow pressure to reduce manually.
- When pressure is reduced, open the lid, and add the shrimp to the soup. Allow the shrimp to cook for about 4 minutes in the heat mode till it turns pink. Your soup is now ready to be served.

Kelp Noodles with Beef Soup

Ingredients

- Sesame Oil- 2 tablespoons
- Sea Salt- 1 teaspoon
- Pepper to season
- 1 inch cubes of stew meat- 2 pounds
- Diced Onions-1
- Minced Garlic- 2 cloves
- Minced Ginger- 3 tablespoons
- Beef bone broth- 3 cups
- Dry Sherry- ½ cup
- Soy Sauce- ¼ cup
- Broccoli florets, peeled and diced- 2 florets
- Cabbage chiffonade- ½
- Kelp Noodles- 2 packages
- Sriracha to taste

Procedure

- Set the cooker to the sauté mode and add the sesame oil.
- Season the meat with salt and pepper a place in the pot. Cook the meat and remember to turn it occasionally. Allow it to brown evenly. Set it aside on a plate.
- Add the onions, carrots, celery and continue to stir. Stir until the vegetables have wilted.
- Now, add the browned meat, ginger, garlic, sherry, soy sauce and broth.
- Close the lid, lock it into place, close the vent and set timer for 20 minutes.
- When time is up, allow pressure to reduce naturally
- When pressure is reduced, open the lid and remove.
- Serve it over the cooked Kelp Noodles. Add a dash of sriracha for that extra flavor.

Veggie Soup with spicy Chicken Chunks

<u>Ingredients</u>

- Frozen Chicken breasts- 1 lb.
- Quartered Onion -1
- Chopped Carrot-1
- Chopped Celery- 1 stalk
- Diced garlic- 2 teaspoons
- Chopped Zucchini- 2
- Potatoes quartered with skin on -2
- Parmesan Recipe Starters- 1 Can
- Italian Dressing – 1 teaspoon
- Ground Flaxseed- 1 teaspoon
- Pepper to taste.

<u>Procedure</u>

- Place all the ingredients except salt and pepper in the pressure cooker.
- Stir the ingredients together.
- Close the lid, lock it into place, close the vent and set timer for 12 minutes. (in rice mode, if possible)
- When time is up, allow pressure to reduce naturally
- When pressure is reduced, open the lid and shred the chicken breasts as required.
- Now add the salt and pepper and allow the cooker to idle on the 'stay warm' mode for about 30 minutes.

You can serve the dish with whole grain rolls.

Refreshing Tomato Bisque

<u>Ingredients</u>

- Tomatoes- 1 pound
- Water- As required
- Salt and Pepper to season
- Oregano to season
- Basil to season.

<u>Procedure</u>

- Cut the tomatoes into halves or quarters without peeling.
- Place it in the inner liner pot.
- Add 2 cups of water.
- Close the lid, lock it into place, close the vent and set timer for 8 minutes.
- When time is up, allow pressure to reduce manually
- When pressure is reduced, open the lid and take the tomatoes out and blend them into a smooth consistency using an immersion blender.
- Add some salt, pepper and oregano and mix well.

Garnish it with basil leaves and serve with some fresh bread on the side.

Coconut Soup with Butternut Squash

<u>Ingredients</u>

- Peeled, seeded and cubed butternut squash- 1 large
- Finely diced onion- 1
- Finely chopped ginger- 1 inch
- Finely chopped garlic- 2 cloves
- Coconut Milk- 1 can
- Salt to taste
- Lemon Juice- 2 tablespoons
- Curry Powder- 1 ½ teaspoons
- Turmeric- ½ teaspoons
- Olive oil- 2 tablespoons

<u>Procedure</u>

Set cooker on the heat or sauté mode. Heat some olive oil at the base of the cooker and sauté the ginger and garlic in it and add the rest of the ingredients except the lemon juice.

- Set the cooker for 10 minutes and lock the lid.
- The pressure must be released naturally. Remove content.
- Using an immersion blender, make a smooth paste.
- Add a dash of lemon juice and serve hot.

The Lazy Hungarian Soup

<u>Ingredients</u>

- Round Beef Steak- 1 ½ pounds
- Cauliflower, Cabbage and Broccoli- 1 cup mixed
- Carrots- 3 large
- Sliced Red Pepper- 1
- Celery Stalks- 4
- Onion- 1
- Potatoes- 4
- Soy Sauce- ¼ Cup
- Hungarian paprika- 3 teaspoons
- Tomato Juice- 1 Quart
- Water- 2 Cups

<u>Procedure</u>

- There is no need to cut the vegetables. Just throw them in the pot along with the seasoning and the beef steak.
- Close the lid, lock it into place, close the vent and set timer for 35 minutes. (in meat mode if possible)
- When time is up, allow pressure to reduce manually.
- Open the lid and take the steak and the vegetables out. You can blend the vegetables if you want a thicker soup. Or else, just strain the liquid out and use the veggies to make another soup.
- The beef steak must be cut into small pieces and added back to the broth.
- Now shift the program of your electric cooker to the Sauté 'or Heat mode and let the broth simmer.
- You can serve the soup with bread.

Tip: This soup goes really well with a side of dumplings.

Pork and Clam Chowder

Ingredients

- Salt Pork- ¼ lb.
- Onions- 3 large
- Carrot- 1 small
- Potatoes- 4 lbs.
- Crushed Tomatoes- 1 Can
- Clams- 1 Bushel
- Clam Broth
- Celery- 4 stalks
- Egyptian Onions-3 tablespoons
- Lavage- 3 tablespoons
- Oyster Sauce- 3 tablespoons
- Water

Procedure

- Dice the salt pork and make it crisp by rendering it down. You can either leave the crisp pork in or you can take it out and add it while serving.
- Chop the vegetables and place them in the pot of your pressure cooker.
- Add enough water to cover all the ingredients and go a little over them.
- Close the lid, lock it into place, close the vent and set timer for 15 minutes.
- When time is up, allow pressure to reduce naturally.
- When pressure is reduced, open the lid. You can serve the soup with some corn bread.

Tip: In case the soup is too watery, add a bit of corn flour or some Arrow root to thicken it.

Minestrone Soup in Minutes

Ingredients

- Organic chicken broth- 2 aseptic containers
- Sliced Organic Carrots- 5
- Chopped Onion- 1 whole
- Wheat noodles- 1 cup
- Cubed Golden Potatoes- 6
- Organic Diced Tomato in its own juice- 1 can
- Sliced Organic Celery- 2 stalks
- Chopped Broccoli- 1 crown

Procedure

- Add all the ingredients to the pot of the electric pressure cooker.
- Do not fill the pot to the top.
- Close the lid, lock it into place, close the vent and set timer for 20 minutes.
- When time is up, allow pressure to reduce naturally.
- When pressure is reduced, open the lid. You must make sure that the noodles are fully cooked.

Add the seasoning as per your requirement. You can even add a dash of hot sauce before serving the soup.

Warm rolls go perfectly with this soup!

Fresh Veggies and Ox tail Soup

Ingredients

- Oxtail cut into 1 inch chunks- 2 pounds
- Tomatoes cut into pieces- 2
- Peeled and Diced carrots- 2
- Diced celery- 1 Stalk
- Vegetable Oil- 2 tablespoons
- Tomato Paste- 2 tablespoons
- Salt- 2 teaspoons
- Chopped Green Onion- 1
- Ginger- 3 slices
- Black Pepper- ¼ teaspoon
- Wine- ¼ cup
- Water- as required

Procedure

- Place all the ingredients in the pot of your pressure cooker.
- Close the lid, lock it into place, close the vent and set timer for 20 minutes. (in soup mode, if possible)
- When time is up, allow pressure to reduce naturally

 When pressure is reduced, open the lid, your soup is ready to serve. Sprinkle some seasoning over it and serve warm.

Veggie Soup with Spicy Chicken Chunks

Ingredients

- Frozen Chicken breasts- 1 lb.
- Quartered Onion -1
- Chopped Carrot-1
- Chopped Celery- 1 stalk
- Diced garlic- 2 teaspoons
- Chopped Zucchini- 2
- Potatoes quartered with skin on -2
- Parmesan Recipe Starters- 1 Can
- Italian Dressing – 1 teaspoon
- Ground Flaxseed- 1 teaspoon
- Pepper to taste.

Procedure

- Place all the ingredients except salt and pepper in the pressure cooker.
- Stir the ingredients together.
- Close the lid, lock it into place, close the vent and set timer for 12 minutes. (in rice mode, if possible)
- When time is up, allow pressure to reduce naturally
- When pressure is reduced, open the lid and shred the chicken breasts as required.
- Now add the salt and pepper and allow the cooker to idle on the 'stay warm' mode for about 30 minutes.

You can serve the dish with whole grain rolls.

PROTEINS

The most important part of our food is protein. Like they say, proteins are the building blocks of our body. For any growth or repair to occur within our body, proteins are extremely important. But, there is one tiny little problem with proteins. They take a tremendous amount of time to cook. So, we end up using artificial protein sources like protein drinks or protein bars to make up for it. Although artificial sources have not really caused any harm to people, the truth is that, the more organic and natural your food, the healthier your body will be.

Now, for some good news, with a pressure cooker, you can cook any type of protein within a couple of minutes. The most common protein sources are chicken, beef, seafood or lamb. For the vegetarians, beans are the best source of proteins. As most experience cooks know, these foods take the longest time to cook well.

Don't worry! The recipes that have been included in this book will take you by surprise. You will not believe how easy it is to cook even the most dreaded dishes! All you need to do is turn to your handy electric pressure cooker.

Meat Loaf in a Cooker

<u>Ingredients</u>

- Ground Meat- 1 lb.
- Chopped Onion- 1
- Egg- 1
- Drained Mushrooms- Small Can
- Milk- 1 cup
- Water – 1 cup
- Potato- Optional

<u>Topping</u>

- Ketchup- ¾ Cup
- Brown Sugar- 4 Tablespoons

<u>Procedure</u>

- Spray some nonstick spray in the inner pot.
- Mix all the ingredients for the meat loaf. Shape the contents into a round loaf and wrap in tin foil. Add 1 cup of water.

- Close the lid, lock it into place, close the vent and set timer for 15 minutes
- When time is up, allow pressure to reduce naturally.
- When pressure is reduced, open the lid. If meat is not cooked enough for you, set for another 5 minutes.
- Release the pressure naturally and serve.

Shredded and Pulled Barbeque Beef

<u>Ingredients</u>

- Roast Angus Beef- 1 1/3 pounds
- Water or left over stock- 1 cup

<u>For the Sauce</u>

- Low Sugar ketchup- ½ cup
- Honey- 2 teaspoons
- Barbeque seasoning of your choice- ¼ Cup
- Water- ¼ cup

<u>Procedure</u>

- Spray the inner pot with nonstick spray.
- Add the frozen beef roast and the stock into the pot.
- Close the lid, lock it into place, close the vent and set timer for 60 minutes. (in meat mode, if possible)
- Reduce pressure manually. When pressure is reduced, open the lid
- In a separate bowl, mix all the ingredients and keep it aside.
- Turn the pot off and transfer the meat on to a plate.
- Trim all the fat and discard.
- Pull the rest of the meat into chunks.
- Place the pulled beef back in the cooker and pour the BBQ sauce.
- Allow it to cook in the sauté or heat mode for a couple of minutes. Continue to stir the contents.
- As you let the contents cook, pull the meat with forks and let the sauce stick to the meat. This
Should take about 2 minutes.

- Once the pulled beef is ready, spread it over a whole grain hamburger bread.
- Add some mayonnaise based coleslaw and serve with French fries.

Meatloaf with a Special Sweet Glaze

Ingredients
- Lean ground beef- 1 pound
- Crumbled cornbread- 2/3 cup
- Egg White- 1
- Diced Onions- 1
- Sliced Black Olives- 6
- Basil leaves, chopped- 2
- Salt to taste
- Pepper to taste
- Minced Garlic- 1 teaspoon
- Ground Flaxseed- 1 tablespoon
- Ketchup- 2 tablespoons

For the Glaze
- Cane sugar or brown sugar- 1 tablespoon
- Spicy brown mustard- 1 tablespoon
- Ketchup- ¼ cup

Procedure
- Mix all the ingredients other than the glaze ingredients. Shape them by hand and form a loaf.
- In a bowl, stir all the glaze ingredients together and spread over the meatloaf.
- In the pot of the cooker, pour one cup of water and add thetrivet cover with foil.
- On this trivet, place the meatloaf.
- Close the lid, lock it into place, close the vent and set timer for 15minutes. (in meat mode, if possible)
- When time is up, allow pressure to reduce naturally
- When pressure is reduced, open the lid...
- Now remove the meat loaf from the trivet. Check to make sure it is cooked through. If not cook for 5 more minutes. Allow to sit for a few minutes and serve

Kosher Brisket Cooked in Chicken Broth

Ingredients

- Kosher Brisket- 2 pound
- Oil- 2 tablespoons
- Pepper- ½ teaspoon
- Spanish Onion- 1 medium sized
- Red potatoes or regular potatoes- 5
- Baby carrots- 1 cup
- Chicken Broth- 1 ½ cups

Procedure

- Set the cooker to the 'sauté' mode.
- Add 1 tbsp. of oil to caramelize the onions. When the onions are golden brown, take them out of the pot, place in a bowl and set aside.
- Let the cooker stay in the sauté mode.
- Season the brisket with pepper on both sides. You may add salt if required.
- In the cooker, sear the beef.
- Then, throw in the carrots, potatoes and onions.
- Pour the chicken broth over.
- Close the lid, lock it into place, close the vent and set timer for 60 minutes.
- When time is up, allow pressure to reduce naturally.
- When pressure is reduced, open the lid and remove all the vegetables.
- Put the cooker back on sauté mode and reduce the juices around the brisket to half.
- Once this is done, serve with the sides.

Chinese Stew with Beef

Ingredients

- Oil- 1 -2 tablespoons-
- Sliced onions- 1
- Sugar- ½ teaspoons
- Red wine or Sherry- 1 tablespoon
- Cubed Beef round- 2.5 pounds
- Cornstarch- 2 teaspoons
- Smoked Paprika- a pinch
- Garlic powder- 1 – 2 teaspoons
- Salt and pepper to taste
- Beef broth- ½ cup
- Worcestershire sauce- 1 tablespoon
- Mushrooms- 1 can
- Chopped Ginger- 1- 2 teaspoons
- Corn Slurry (I if necessary) – 1 – 2 teaspoons

Procedure

- Set the pressure cooker to heat or sauté mode and sauté onions until soft...
- To the onions, add some sugar, soy sauce and red wine and cook for 30 seconds.
- Pour in the beef broth and the Worcestershire sauce. Give the contents a stir
- Close the lid, lock it into place, close the vent and set timer for 30 minutes. (in meat mode, if possible)
- When time is up, allow pressure to reduce naturally
- When pressure is reduced, open the lid. If the meat is not done, allow it to cook for 5 more minutes.
- When you are sure that the meat is fully done, add the chopped ginger, garlic and mushrooms.
- You may add more salt if required.
- If the gravy needs to be thickened, add some corn starch slurry.
- Allow the contents to sauté for a minute.
- The dish is ready to be served. It goes best with a cup of steamed rice and some stir fried greens and veggies.

Sour Cream and Beef Barley Mushroom Stew

Ingredients

- Stew Beef cut into chunks- 1 lb.
- Chopped Yellow Onion- 1 small
- Beef Broth- 3 cups
- Sliced Mushrooms- 1 cup
- Salt and coarsely ground pepper to taste
- Bay Leaf- 1
- Thyme Sprig- 1
- Tomato paste- 1 teaspoon
- Worcestershire sauce- 1 teaspoon
- Uncooked pearl barley- ½ cup
- Sour Cream- 1 cup
- Chopped Parsley- 1 teaspoon

Procedure

- Place all the ingredients except the cream and parsley in the cooker.
- Close the lid, lock it into place, close the vent and set timer for 30 minutes.
- When time is up, allow pressure to reduce naturally
- When pressure is reduced, open the lid and remove the bay leaf and the sprig of thyme.
- Add salt and pepper if required.
- Mix in about ¾ of the sour cream
- Serve with a sprinkle of parsley and some sour cream.

Tip: If you have the time, brown the meat with some butter and onion before cooking with the rest of the ingredients.

Rosemary Alfredo Fettuccine with Cabernet Short Ribs

<u>Ingredients</u>

- Beef Short ribs- 8
- Salt and pepper to taste
- Canola Oil- 2 tablespoons
- Sliced fennel bulb- ½
- Cabernet Sauvignon- 1 cup
- 1 cup beef broth
- Red wine vinegar- 1 tablespoon
- Olive Oil- 2 tablespoons
- Trimmed watercress- 2 bunches
- Butter- ½ cup
- Heavy Whipping Cream- 1 pint
- Grated Cheese- 2 cups
- Nutmeg- 1 teaspoon
- Chopped Rosemary- 1 tablespoon
- Fettuccine- 1 package

<u>Procedure</u>

- Season the beef ribs with salt and pepper
- In a large skillet, heat the canola oil and add the short ribs. Sear for about 2 minutes on each side.
- Place the seared beef in the pot of the pressure cooker.
- Add fennel, cabernet and beef broth.
- Close the lid, lock it into place, close the vent and set timer for 35 minutes. (in meat mode if possible)
- While the beef is cooking, whisk the red wine vinegar, garlic and olive oil in a small bowl.
- Top it with some water cress and keep it aside.
- Melt the butter on low heat in a medium sauce pan.
- Add the whipping cream and cheese. Allow the cheese to melt fully.
- Add the nutmeg and rosemary and blend well.
- In a large pot, cook the fettuccine in salted water. Strain and mix with the cheese sauce.
- Once the beef is done, release the pressure naturally.

- Serve the beef ribs with fettuccine and the dressed watercress.

Beef Bourguinon

<u>Ingredients</u>

- Boneless Beef Chuck roast chunks- 1 ½ lbs.
- Carrots, cut in chunks- 5
- Mushroom quarters- 8 ounces
- Peeled Pearl onions- 12
- Minced Garlic Cloves – 2
- Bay leaf- 1
- Salt to taste
- Thyme- 2 tablespoons
- Black pepper- ¼ teaspoons
- Dry Red Wine- 2/3 cup
- Tomato Paste- 2 tablespoons
- Whole wheat flour- 2 teaspoons
- Water- ¼ cup

<u>Procedure</u>

- In the pressure cooker, sauté the dry beef until it is evenly brown. Set it aside.
- Similarly, brown the pearl onions
- Add all the ingredients except flour and water and set the cooker. Close the lid, lock it into place, close the vent and set timer for 20 minutes.
- When time is up, allow pressure to reduce naturally
- When pressure is reduced, open the lid. Make a paste with water and flour and pour in.
- Allow this mixture to cook until the sauce thickens.

Serve with rice or bread.

Rolls of Cabbage

Ingredients

- Head of green cabbage- 1
- Hamburger 1 ½ pounds
- Salt- 2 teaspoons
- Pepper to season
- Minute Rice- 1 cup
- Cinnamon- 1 teaspoon
- Crushed tomatoes- 1 can

Procedure

- Allow the cabbage to wilt by dipping it in hot water. Separate the leaves to make the rolls.
- In a large bowl, mix the hamburger, salt, pepper, rice and cinnamon.
- In each leaf place about 2 tablespoons of the mixture and roll. Tuck the ends in.
- Place the rolls in the pressure cooker.
- Pour the canned tomatoes over these rolls.
- Close the lid, lock it into place, close the vent and set timer for 15 minutes.
- When time is up, allow pressure to reduce naturally
- When pressure is reduced, open the lid and remove.

Spicy Swiss Steak

<u>Ingredients</u>

- Thick round steak in serving size pieces- 3 pounds
- Crushed tomatoes- 1 can
- V-8- 1 can
- Worcestershire Sauce- 1 teaspoon
- Beau Monde Seasoning- 1 teaspoon
- Granulated Garlic- 1 teaspoon
- Seasoned Salt- ¼ teaspoon
- Pepper- ¼ teaspoon
- Bay leaves- 2
- Onion cut in chunks- 1
- Celery- 4 stalks
- Chopped Carrots- 1 cup

<u>Procedure</u>

- In a large skillet, brown both sides of the steak lightly.
- Add the can of V8 to the pressure cooker. Now add the steak.
- Mix in the carrots, onion and celery.
- In another bowl, mix the remaining ingredients well and pour over the meat and veggies.
- Close the lid, lock it into place, close the vent and set timer for40 minutes. (in meat mode, if possible)
- When time is up, allow pressure to reduce naturally
- When pressure is reduced, open the lid and remove.

Your dish is ready to be served.

Stew with Oxtail and Veggies

Ingredients

- Oxtails- 5 lbs.
- Salt and pepper- to taste
- Chopped and peeled onion- 1
- Chopped Carrot- 3
- Chopped Celery- 3 stalks
- Peeled and chopped garlic- 1 clove
- Parsley- 1 bunch
- Red Wine- 2 cups
- Chopped Tomatoes- 1 cup
- Water- 1 cup
- Sugar to taste

Procedure

- Season the oxtails with salt and pepper on both sides.
- Place it in the cooker.
- Pour the remaining ingredients over the oxtails and then add water and wine.
- Close the lid, lock it into place, close the vent and set timer for 40 minutes.
- When time is up, allow pressure to reduce naturally
- When pressure is reduced, open the lid and remove.
- Add some more salt and pepper, if required and serve.

The Hot Hurry Curry

Ingredients

- Yellow Curry Paste- 1 tablespoon
- Chicken Broth- 1 cup
- Beef- 1 lb.
- Fish Sauce- 2 tablespoons
- Garlic- 2 cloves
- Lime leaves- 2
- Ginger- 1 inch piece
- Carrot- 1da
- Onion- 1
- Potato- 1
- Red pepper- 1
- Coconut milk- 1 can

Procedure

- Add all the ingredients to the pressure cooker. Make sure you chop all the vegetables.
- Close the lid, lock it into place, close the vent and set timer for 20 minutes.
- When time is up, allow pressure to reduce naturally
- When pressure is reduced, open the lid and remove.
- Serve with some rice or noodles.

Tip: You can add bamboo shoots and cilantro for some additional flavor

CHICKEN

Enchiladas with Corn and Chicken

Ingredients

- Frozen Chicken Breasts- 1 pound
- Water- 2 cups
- Green chili Enchilada Sauce- 1 can
- Neufchatel Cheese- 1 packet
- Onions, green peppers and hot peppers- ½ each
- Chopped Spinach- 1 cup
- 6 inch yellow tortillas- 12
- Grated Cheddar Cheese- 3 Ounces

Procedure

- Place the frozen chicken breasts in the cooker. Add 2 cups of water and close the lid, lock it into place, close the vent and set timer for 15 minutes.
- When time is up, allow pressure to reduce naturally
- When pressure is reduced, open the lid and take out the excess water.
- Keeping the chicken in the pot, shred it using a large fork.
- Add the Neufchatel cheese, onions, peppers, spinach and the enchilada sauce.
- Set the cooker to the sauté or heat mode to soften the cheese little. You must sauté the contents for not more than 1 minute.
- Preheat and oven to 400 degrees. In a baking pan, place the corn tortillas filled with the chicken and the mixture prepared before.
- Dribble the remaining enchilada sauce and sprinkle the cheddar cheese over it. Cover the baking tray with aluminum foil.
- After 10 minutes in the oven, remove the foil and continue to cook till the cheese melts completely.

Your dish is ready to be served.

Sweet and SpicyCHICKEN

Ingredients

- Boneless chicken thighs- 8
- Glaze
- Chili powder- 2 teaspoons
- Onion powder- ½ teaspoon
- Coriander- ½ teaspoon
- Cumin- 1 teaspoon
- Honey- ½ cup
- Cider or Balsamic Vinegar-1 tablespoon
- ½ cup chicken broth

Procedure

- Preheat an oven to 400 degrees
- Place the chicken in the pressure cooker pot. Add ½ chicken broth...
- Close the lid, lock it into place, close the vent and set timer for 15 minutes. (in poultry mode, if possible)
- When time is up, allow pressure to reduce naturally
- When pressure is reduced, open the lid place the chicken pieces in a baking sheet. Now place the chicken in the oven for about 15 minutes till the skin is fully crispy.
- Take the chicken out of the oven and let it cool a little.
- In a bowl, strain the chicken broth. Place the broth back in the cooker and set the program to 'sauté' or heat.
- Add the vinegar, honey and other seasoning to the broth. Let it simmer until the sauce thickens. This should take about 15 minutes. Make sure you stir continuously.
- You will know that your broth is ready when it gets the consistency of syrup.
- Pour this sauce over the chicken and serve with rice.

Chicken and Mushroom Stew

Ingredients

- Cooked and seasoned roast chicken- 1 whole
- Chopped Celery- 1 cup
- Chopped Mushrooms- 1 cup
- Chopped Onion- 1
- Chopped Carrots- 1 cup

Procedure

- Shred the chicken meat and place in the pot of the cooker.
- Place all the vegetables in.
- Add 2 cups of broth.
- Close the lid, lock it into place, close the vent and set timer for 10 minutes.
- When time is up, allow pressure to reduce naturally
- When pressure is reduced, open the lid and remove.

Serve with rice or pasta.

Tomatillo Sauce with Chunky Chicken

Ingredients

- Olive Oil- 2 teaspoons
- Diced Onion- 1 large
- Crushed Garlic- 1 clove
- Skinless chicken thighs- 2.5 pounds
- Green Chilies - 1 Can
- Cilantro- a handful
- Tomatillos- 16 ounces
- Salt and pepper to taste
- Garbanzo Beans- 8 ounces
- Rice- 16 ounces
- Cheddar Cheese- 16 ounces
- Chopped Tomatoes- 200 ml
- Black Olives- 100 ml

Procedure

- Set Pressure Cooker to heat, add olive oil and sauté the onions till they are translucent.
- Add the garlic, chilies, cilantro and tomatillo.
- Season with salt and pepper
- Add the chicken, beans and rice. Lock the lid and set the timer for 12 minutes (poultry mode is possible)
- Release the pressure naturally.
- Once you remove the lid, shred the chicken in the pot. Put cooker on heat or sauté mode. And add the cheese.
- Once the cheese has melted over the meat, your dish is ready to be served.

Indian Chicken Curry

Ingredients

- Chicken- 1
- Coriander seeds- 1 teaspoon
- Spanish onion- 1
- Grated Ginger- 1 teaspoon
- Garlic Powder- 1 teaspoon
- Garam Masala Powder- 2 teaspoons
- Chili Powder- 1 teaspoon
- Oil- To tablespoons
- Salt to taste
- Cilantro to Garnish
- 1 cup water

For the Marinade

- Chili Powder- 1 teaspoon
- Turmeric Powder- ½ teaspoon
- Ginger Powder- 2 teaspoons
- Coriander Powder- 2 teaspoons
- Juice of 1 lemon
- Salt to taste.

Procedure

- Marinade the chicken, cover and refrigerate for about 1 hour.
- Meanwhile, set the cooker to sauté or heat mode.
- Add the coriander seeds. Let the cook till they pop.
- Now add chopped onion and sauté till it is translucent.
- Add the garlic powder, garam masala, ginger powder and chili powder. Sauté for a minute.
- Add the tomatoes and cook them till they are soft.

- Add the marinated chicken and continue to sauté
- Add water and salt.
- Close the lid, lock it into place, close the vent and set timer for 20 minutes. (in poultry mode)
- When time is up, allow pressure to reduce naturally
- When pressure is reduced, open the lid and remove.
- Serve the dish with some rice.

Lemon and Paprika Chicken

Ingredients

- Chopped Cilantro -1/4 cup
- Paprika- 1 tablespoon
- Ground Cumin- 2 teaspoons
- Salt to taste
- Turmeric powder- ½ teaspoon
- Finely Chopped Garlic- 2 cloves
- Boneless chickenbreasts- 2 pounds
- Water- ½ cup
- Lemon juice- ¼ cup
- Chicken bouillon cube- 1
- Sliced Calamata Olives- 1 small can

Procedure

- Prepare some steamed white rice in the cooker as per directions.
- Meanwhile, in a food processor, mix the paprika, cumin, cilantro, salt, turmeric, ginger and garlic.
- Marinate the chicken pieces with this cilantro paste.
- Your rice should be done by now. Remove and set aside.
- Place the chicken in the cooker
- Add water and lemon juice.
- Toss in the olives
- Close the lid, lock it into place, close the vent and set timer for 12 minutes.
- When time is up, allow pressure to reduce naturally
When pressure is reduced, open the lid and remove.

Peasant Soup with Cabbage

Ingredients

- Chicken Broth
- Diced Onion – 1
- Smashed and Diced Garlic- 1 clove
- Baking Potatoes, peeled and quartered - 2 large
- Cut tomato -1
- Bay Leaf- 1
- Shredded Cabbage- 3 to 4 cups
- Rinsed and drained sauerkraut
- 1 - Ham or Garlic Sausage
- Diced Carrots- 1 cup

Procedure

- In the pot of the pressure cooker, pour a little oil and choose the Heat or Sauté option.
- Put in the onions and celery and cook till the onion is translucent.
- Add the garlic and sauté.
- Add the broth into the pot with the sautéed vegetables and the rest of the ingredients.
- Place in soup mode if possible.
- Close the lid, lock it into place, close the vent and set timer for 20 minutes.
- When time is up, allow pressure to reduce naturally
- When pressure is reduced, open the lid and remove.
- Garnish with parsley and serve.

Pumpkin Seed Wild Rice with Pot Chicken and Cherries

Ingredients

- Balsamic Vinegar- 1 cup
- Evaporated Palm Sugar- ½ cup
- Molasses- 1 tablespoon
- Melted butter- ¼ cup
- Peeled and quartered orange- 1
- Julienned onion- 1
- Chicken thighs- 12
- Sea Salt- ¼ teaspoon
- Rosemary- 4 sprigs
- Pitted and halved Bing Cherries- 1 ½ cups

For the Wild Rice

- Vegetable Stock- 4 cups
- Wild Rice- 1 1/3 cup
- Butter- ¼ cup
- Minced Onion-1
- Diced plum tomatoes- 2
- Toasted Pumpkin seeds- ½ cup
- Salt to taste

Procedure

- In the pot of the cooker, add the balsamic vinegar, palm sugar, molasses, butter, onion and orange. Mix the contents well.
- Now add the chicken, rosemary and salt. Stir till the chicken is fully coated.
- Now mix the cherries in.
- Close the lid, lock it into place, close the vent and set timer for 20 minutes.

- While the chicken is cooking, in a separate pot, cook the wild rice in vegetable stock for 50 minutes.
- In a skillet, caramelize onions in butter. Now add tomatoes and sauté. Add this to the rice.
- In a separate pan, cook cherries and sauté till it becomes soft and juicy.
- Mix in the cherries and the toasted pumpkin seeds with the rice.
- Release pressure naturally. Remove contents from the pressure cooker and serve over rice...

Sour Lemon Chicken

Ingredients

- Chicken breasts- 2
- Olive Oil- 2 teaspoons
- Flour- 2 teaspoons
- Sliced Lemon- ½
- Brown Sugar- ½ teaspoon
- Ketchup- 1 ½ teaspoon
- While vinegar- 1 ½ teaspoon
- Lemon Zest- ½ teaspoon
- Lemon juice from ½ lemon
- Lemon concentrate- 1/3 cup

Procedure

- Cover the chicken with salt and flour.
- In the pot, pour some oil.
- Arrange the lemon slices at the bottom and place the chicken over it.
- Turn the cooker to theheat sauté mode and brown the chicken on both sides.
- Make a sauce with the remaining ingredients and pour it over the chicken.
- Close the lid, lock it into place, close the vent and set timer for 10 minutes.
- When time is up, allow pressure to reduce naturally

When pressure is reduced, open the lid and remove.

Easy Chicken Broth

<u>Ingredients</u>

- Chicken parts- 3 pounds
- Vegetable trimmings- 1 quart zip bag full
- Salt and Pepper to season
- Bay Leaf- 1
- Water

<u>Procedure</u>

- In the cooker pot, fill water and add the chicken and vegetables.
- Sprinkle the seasoning and add the bay leaves.
- The water must go at least 2 inches above the contents.
- Now place the lid on the pressure cooker and set timer for 30 minutes.
- Allow the steam to release naturally after the cooker beeps.
- Strain the contents of in the cooker and your broth is ready to be used.

Macaroni and Cheese with Chicken

Ingredients

- Chicken Tenders- 1 pound
- Rigatoni pasta- 3 cups
- Chicken Stock- 3 cups
- Chopped Onion- 1 small
- Chopped Celery- 3 ribs
- Peeled and chopped carrots
- Hot wing sauce- 2/3 cup
- Ranch Seasoning- 1 tablespoon
- Light Whipped Cream- ½ cup
- Sharp Cheddar- 1 cup
- Mozzarella Cheese- 1 cup, shredded.
- Feta Cheese- ½ Cup

Procedure

- Place the chicken tenders, the vegetables, the wing sauce, the ranch seasoning and the pasta in the pot of the pressure cooker.
- Pour the broth over the contents.
- Stir the contents and lock the lid.
- Set timer for 10 minutes. (in rice mode if possible)
- Once the cooker beeps, quick release the pressure and stir the cheese in till it dissolves completely.
- Now, add the cheddar, Swiss cheese and the feta cheese and let it dissolve.

Your dish is ready to be served.

The Sloppy Chicken Soup

<u>Ingredients</u>

- Chicken thighs and legs- 6
- Hot Chili Beans- 1 can
- Chicken Broth
- Garlic powder or minced garlic- 1 teaspoon
- Chopped Onion- 1
- Chopped potatoes- 3 medium
- Rice or pasta of your choice- 1 cup
- Peas- 1 can
- Turkey Bacon, cut up- 3 slices.

<u>Procedure</u>
- Place all the contents in the pressure cooker pot.
- Close the lid, lock it into place, close the vent and set timer for 10 minutes.
- When time is up, allow pressure to reduce naturally
- When pressure is reduced, open the lid and remove.
- Season with salt and pepper and serve.

Chicken baked with Salt 'n' Garlic

Ingredients

- Chicken- 1 medium sized
- Minced Green Onion- 1
- Minced Ginger- 1 small
- Sugar- 2 tablespoons
- Salt- 2 teaspoons
- Soy Sauce- 2 teaspoons
- Cooking wine- ½ cup

Procedure

- Season the chicken inside and outside with 1 teaspoon of salt and sugar.
- In the inner pot of the cooker, rub 1 teaspoon of salt on the bottom
- Place the chicken, soy sauce and the wine in the electric pressure cooker.
- Close the lid, lock it into place, close the vent and set timer for 10 minutes. (in stew mode or meat mode)
- When time is up, allow pressure to reduce quickly
- When pressure is reduced, open the lid and remove.
- Turn the chicken and cook again similarly for 10 more minutes.
- Your chicken is now ready. Cut it into pieces and serve.

On the side, mix ginger, chicken oil and green onion to make the dipping sauce.

Arroz Con Pollo

Ingredients

- Olive Oil- ¼ cup
- Chopped Garlic- 3 cloves
- Sea Salt- 1 tablespoon
- Fresh Ground Pepper- ½ teaspoon
- Minced Oregano- 3 tablespoons
- Ground Cumin- 2 teaspoons
- Chicken- 1 whole
- Fresh Lime Juice- 2 tablespoons

For the Sofrito

- Garlic Cloves- 3-4
- Chopped Yellow onion- ½ medium
- Green Bell Pepper, chopped and seeded- ½
- Cilantro- 1 handful
- Sea Salt- ½ teaspoon
- Ground Black Pepper- ¼ teaspoon

For the Rice

- Coconut Oil- 2 tablespoons
- Diced Yellow Onion- 1
- Red Bell Pepper, diced- 1
- Ground Cumin- 1 teaspoon
- Minced Fresh Oregano -1 tablespoon
- Diced Tomatoes- 1 can
- Organic Chicken Stock- 5 cups
- Brown rice- 3 cups
- Sea Salt0 ¼ teaspoon

- Spanish Olives- 1 ½ cups
- Olive Brine- 2 tablespoons

Procedure

- For the Marinade:
- Mix the olive oil, garlic, sea salt, oregano, cumin powder, salt, pepper and the lime in a bowl.
- Coat the chicken evenly with the marinade
- Allow it to sit for an hour or overnight

- For the Sofrito
- Mix all the ingredients of the sofrito and process in a blender until smooth.
- For the Rice
- Set the cooker on sauté mode.
- Melt the coconut oil and brown the marinated chicken in the oil.
- When the chicken is golden brown on both sides, transfer to another plate and cut up.
- In the pot of the cooker, sauté the onions, cumin, red bell pepper and the oregano. Allow the contents to become tender.
- Now, stir in the sofrito and toss for about 3 minutes. If there is any marinade that is left over, add it to the pot.
- Stir in the olives, rice and the stock.
- Add the chicken pieces to the pot.
- Close the lid, lock it into place, close the vent and set timer for 20minutes. (in meat mode, if possible)
- When time is up, allow pressure to reduce naturally
- When pressure is reduced, open the lid and remove.
- Your dish is ready to be served.

Fried Multigrain Brown Rice

Ingredients

- Multi grain rice- 3 cups
- Water – 1/2 cups
- Diced chicken – 1 cup
- Sliced Scallions- ¼ cup
- Julienned Carrots- 1 cup
- Olive Oil or butter – 2 tablespoons
- Soy Sauce – 1- 2 tablespoons

Procedure

- Add all the ingredients to the pressure cooker
- Close the lid, lock it into place, close the vent and set timer for 10 minutes. (in multigrain mode, if possible)
- When time is up, allow pressure to reduce naturally
- When pressure is reduced, open the lid and remove.
- Fluff the rice and Serve Warm.

DUCK

Duck 'n' Veggies

<u>Ingredients</u>

- Duck- 1 medium sized
- Diced Cucumber- 1
- Diced Carrots- 2
- Cooking wine- 1 tablespoon
- Water- 2 cups
- Chopped Ginger- 1 inch
- Salt- 2 teaspoons

<u>Procedure</u>

- Place all the ingredients in the pot of a pressure cooker.
- Set the cooker to meat or stew mode.
- Close the lid, lock it into place, close the vent and set timer for 15 minutes.
- When time is up, allow pressure to reduce naturally
- When pressure is reduced, open the lid and remove.

Potato and Braised Duck

Ingredients

- Duck chopped into chunks- 1 whole
- Potatoes, cubed- 1
- Garlic, minced- 4 cloves
- Green Onions- 2, cut into 2 inch pieces
- Soy Sauce- 4 tablespoons
- Sugar- 4 tablespoons
- Sherry Wine- 4 tablespoons
- Salt to taste
- Water- ¼ cup

Procedure

- Set the pot to sauté mode and heat it for a while.
- Sear the chunks of the duck keeping the skin side down.
- When the duck is golden brown, stir in all the ingredients besides the potato.
- Close the lid, lock it into place, close the vent and set timer for 20 minutes.
- When time is up, allow pressure to reduce naturally
  - When pressure is reduced, open the lid andstir in the potato cubes.
- Set it to heat mode and allow it to cook for 5 more minutes with lid off..
- Serve with bread or some rice.

Herbs and Spice Duck Breast

<u>Ingredients</u>

- Duck breast halves- 2 large
- Salt- 1 teaspoon
- Minced Garlic- 2 teaspoons
- Ground Black pepper- ½ teaspoon
- Dry Thyme- 1/3 teaspoon
- Peppercorn- 1/3 teaspoon
- Vegetable oil- 1 tablespoon
- Peeled, cored and mashed apricot- 1 large

<u>Procedure</u>

- Clean the duck breast pieces and rub all the seasoning on it.
- Cover it and refrigerate for 2 hours.
- Rinse the spices and place the duck breasts in a Ziploc bag. Make sure the seal is airtight.
- In the pressure cooker pot, pour water up to the 7 cup mark.
- Keep the lid open and turn the cooker on. Press the keep warm button and let the water heat for about 20 minutes. Then place the Ziploc bag in the water for about 40 minutes.
- Remove the pieces from the water and pat the duck breasts dry.
- In a non stick pan, sear the skin side of the duck with a tablespoon of vegetable oil until it is golden. Turn it over and cook the other side well.
- Mix the apricots and sugar to make the apricot sauce.
- Slice the cooked duck and serve with apricot sauce.

PORK

Bahn Mi Sliders

<u>Ingredients</u>

<u>For Pickled Vegetables</u>

- Peeled Baby Carrots- ½ pound
- Radishes- ½ pound
- Peeled Ginger- 1 large chunk
- Water- ½ cup
- Cider Vinegar- 1 cup
- Sugar- 3 tablespoons
- Salt- 1 tablespoon

<u>For the Pork</u>

- Pork tenderloin- 2 lb.
- Water- 1 cup
- Fish Sauce- 3 tablespoons
- Soy Sauce- 2 tablespoons
- Maple syrup- 2 tablespoons
- Brown Sugar- 1 tablespoon
- Sesame Oil- 1 teaspoon
- Minced Garlic- 2 cloves
- Minced Ginger- 1 inch piece
- Finely Chopped Scallion- 1
- Freshly ground pepper- ½ teaspoon

<u>For Seasoning and Garnishing</u>

- Hawaiian Dinner Rolls

-     Mayonnaise- 1 cup
-     Lettuce leaves- 12
-     Sriracha Sauce- to taste

Procedure

- **For the Pickled Vegetables**

-     Julienne Ginger, Carrots and Radishes.
-     In a sauce pan, mix the water, vinegar, sugar and salt. When it begins to boil, remove from heat.
-     Add the julienned vegetables and allow it to cool. Then refrigerate till you serve.

- **For the Pork**

-     Cut the pork into chunks and pat dry.
-     In the pressure cooker pot, place the pork chunks with the remaining ingredient.
-     Close the lid, lock it into place, close the vent and set timer for 30 minutes.
-     When time is up, allow pressure to reduce naturally
-     When pressure is reduced, open the lid
-     Remove the meat and transfer to a cutting board. Allow it to cool.
-     Shred the meat using two forks. If there is any liquid remaining in the pot pour it over the Meat.
-     Cut open a roll and smear mayonnaise on both sides. Top with drained picked vegetables and pork. Sprinkle the seasoning and serve.

Lotus Soup with Pork Ribs

<u>Ingredients</u>

- Pork Ribs- 1 pound
- Fresh Lotus Root- 8 ounces
- Ginger- 3 slices
- Salt- 2 teaspoons
- Water- 6 cups

<u>Procedure</u>

- Place all the ingredients in the pot of the pressure cooker.
- Close the lid, lock it into place, close the vent and set timer for 20 minutes.
- When time is up, allow pressure to reduce naturally
- When pressure is reduced, open the lid and remove ribs.
- Marinade with your favorite sauce and put ribs in broiler for 20 minutes.
- Serve warm

Hearty Soup with Greens and Pork

<u>Ingredients</u>

- Ground Pork- 3 lbs.
- Fresh Kale- 1 lb.
- Low Fat Chicken Broth- 3 cups
- Red Onion- 1
- Poultry Seasoning Powder- 1 tablespoon
- Garlic Salt- 1 ½ teaspoon

<u>Procedure</u>

- Chop the kale leaves and the onion pieces.
- Pour the chicken broth into the cooker and add the poultry seasoning powder and garlic salt. Add the pork and mix well.
- Close the lid, lock it into place, close the vent and set timer for10 minutes.
- When time is up, allow pressure to reduce naturally
- When pressure is reduced, open the lid and remove.
- Serve with corn tortillas

Pork Carnitas

Ingredients

- Ground ancho chili powder- 1 tablespoon
- Ground Chipotle Chili Powder- 2 teaspoons
- Ground Cumin- 2 teaspoons
- Coriander- 1 teaspoon
- Oregano-1/2 teaspoon
- Pork Shoulder Roast- 3- 4 pounds
- Coconut Oil- 2 tablespoons
- Beer- 1 bottle
- Oranges – 2 large
- Quartered Onion- 1
- Garlic Cloves- 3
- Bay Leaves- 2

Procedure

- In a small bowl, mix ancho chili powder, cumin, coriander, oregano and salt.
- Take the pork out of the netting and cut into 2 inch cubes. Rub the spice mixture evenly on the pork.
- Set the pressure cooker to the sauté mode and melt the coconut oil. Brown the meat evenly and set aside. Add orange juice and beer to the pressure cooker pot. If there are any brown bits stuck to the bottom of your pan, scrape it out. Then add garlic, onion and bay leaves to the pot. Place the meats over these ingredients.
- Close the lid, lock it into place, close the vent and set timer for 30 minutes.
- When time is up, allow pressure to reduce manually
When pressure is reduced, open the lid and remove.
- Let the cooking liquid simmer till it thickens and reduces by half.
- Shred the meat using two forks.
- In a sheet pan, place the shredded meat and pour the reduced cooking liquid over it. Broil this meat till it is crisp.

- You can serve it with salsa and hot tortillas.

Pork Belly Chinese Style

Ingredients

- Sliced Pork Belly- 2 lbs.
- Soy Sauce- ½ Cup
- Cane Sugar- 1-2 teaspoons
- Chinese Cooking wine- 3 tablespoons
- Star Anise- 4
- Pepper Powder- 1-2 teaspoons
- Water- 2 cups
- Fresh Ginger- 4-5 slices
- Sliced Garlic- 6 cloves

Procedure

- Heat a large sauce pan and sear all sides of the pork belly. You should sear each side for about 2 minutes.
- Reduce the heat and add the ginger and garlic. Sauté in the pork fat for about 5 minutes.
- Now, transfer all the ingredients to the pressure cooker.
- Close the lid, lock it into place, close the vent and set timer for 30 minutes.
- When time is up, allow pressure to reduce naturally
- When pressure is reduced, open the lid and remove.
- Your dish is done when the pork almost falls apart with the touch of a fork.

Soy Bean Soup with Pork Feet

<u>Ingredient</u>

- Green Onion, white part- 2
- Green Onion Leaves minced
- Pork Feet- 2 Pounds
- Salt- 2 teaspoons
- Water- 6 cups

<u>Procedure</u>

- Place all the ingredients apart from the green onion leaves into the pressure cooker pot.
- Close the lid, lock it into place, close the vent and set timer for 20 minutes.
- When time is up, allow pressure to reduce naturally
- When pressure is reduced, open the lid and remove.
- Garnish with green shallots and green onion leaves and serve.

Pork Ribs BBQ

Ingredients

- Pork Ribs- 2 racks
- BBQ Sauce- 2 cups
- Water- 1 cup
- Red Onions, peeled, cut in half- 2
- Peeled and Cut Carrots- 4

Procedure

- Cut the ribs and place them in the cooker
- Add half the BBQ sauce and water and close the lid
- Set to 'meat' mode and cook for 15 minutes.
- Allow the pressure to release normally.
- Take the ribs out and set aside.
- In the pressure cooker pot place the onions and the carrots with the remaining sauce.
- Close the lid, lock it into place, close the vent and set timer for 10 minutes.
- When time is up, allow pressure to reduce naturally
- When pressure is reduced, open the lid and remove.
- Serve sauce with the BBQ ribs.

FISH

Tuna and Capers on Pasta

Ingredients

- Olive Oil- 1 tablespoon
- Garlic- 1 clove
- Anchovies- 3
- Tomato Puree- 2 cups
- Salt to taste
- Fusilli Pasta- 16 Oz
- Tuna- 2 cans
- Capers- 2 tablespoons

Procedure

- Preheat the electric cooker on sauté mode.
- On heat mode, heat some oil. Sauté the anchovies and garlic till the anchovies start to disintegrate.
- Add tomato puree to this mixture. Mix well.
- Now add the raw pasta and the tuna.
- Mix till the pasta is coated evenly.
- Close the lid.
- Set the timer to 5 minutes.
- When the cycle is complete, quick release the pressure and open lid.
- Sprinkle capers and serve.

Healthy Mediterranean Fish

Ingredients

- Fish Fillets- 4
- Cherry Tomatoes- 1 lb.
- Salt Cured Olives- 1 cup
- Pickled capers- 2 tablespoons
- Olive Oil
- Pressed Garlic- 1 clove
- Salt and Pepper

Procedure

- In a heat proof bowl, place the cherry tomatoes and the thyme.
- Now place the fish filets over the tomatoes.
- Sprinkle with garlic, olive oil and salt
- Place the dish inside the pressure cooker.
- Close the lid, lock it into place, close the vent and set timer for 6 minutes.
- When time is up, allow pressure to reduce naturally
- When pressure is reduced, open the lid and remove.
- Your dish is ready to be served.

POTATOES

Sweet Potatoes baked in Olive Oil

<u>Ingredients</u>

- Large Sweet Potatoes- 3
- Water- ½ cup
- Extra Virgin Olive Oil- 1 tablespoon.

<u>Procedure</u>

- Wash and scrub the potatoes and coat with olive oil.
- Wrap them in aluminum foil.
- Pour ½ cup of water in the pot and set the potatoes on the trivet.
- Close the lid and set timer for10 minutes.
- Release pressure manually...
- You can top the potatoes with Greek yogurt or butter and serve.

Hearty Potato Soup

<u>Ingredients</u>

- Potatoes, peeled and cut- 2 pounds
- Baby Carrots sliced- ¾ cup
- Creamy Roasted Garlic Recipe Starters- 1 can
- Chopped Celery- ½ cup
- Fresh Baby Spinach- ½ cup
- Chopped Onions- 1 cup
- Broth- 2 Cups
- Crushed Red Pepper- 1/8 teaspoon
- Paprika- 1/8th teaspoon
- Ground Flax and Chia seeds- 1 tablespoon
- Salt- ½ teaspoon
- Grated Sharp Cheddar
- Basil Leaves to garnish

<u>Procedure</u>

- Add all the ingredients except the salt and grated cheese to the pressure cooker. Stir well.
- Close the lid, lock it into place, close the vent and set timer for 25 minutes.
- When time is up, allow pressure to reduce quickly (manually)
- When pressure is reduced, open the lid
- Insert and immersion blender into the pot and pulse it till the soup is thick with pieces of potato and carrot.
- Garnish with salt and pepper and serve warm.

Garlic Greek Yogurt and Mashed Potatoes

<u>Ingredients</u>

- Peeled Baking Potatoes- 1 ½ pounds
- Water- ½ cup
- Butter- ½ tablespoon
- Skim Milk- ½ cup
- Greek Yoghurt- 1.2 cup
- Minced Garlic- ½ teaspoon
- Pepper- For Seasoning
- Cheddar Cheese to Garnish

<u>Procedure</u>

- Pour ½ cup of water into the pressure cooker pot.
- Set the potatoes on a trivet and place in the pot. Close the lid, lock it into place, close the vent and set timer for 15 minutes.
- When time is up, allow pressure to reduce naturally
- When pressure is reduced, open the lid and remove.
- The potatoes should soft in the middle.
- Turn the pot off and remove the trivet.
- While the potatoes are still hot, add some butter. Pour half the skim milk, yogurt and garlic over the potatoes.
- Smash the potatoes till it reaches the consistency you like.
- Garnish with salt and pepper and serve.

The Comfort Potato Soup

<u>Ingredients</u>

- Diced Onion- 1
- Nitrite Free bacon- 2 slices
- Minced Garlic- 1 teaspoon
- Olive Oil- ½ teaspoon
- Chicken Broth- 1 + 2 cups
- Peeled and Chopped Potatoes- 2 ½ lbs.
- Carrots Diced- 2
- Dried parsley- 1 tablespoon
- Dried red pepper flakes- to season
- Italian Seasoning- to season
- Evaporated Milk- 12 ounce
- Salt to taste
- Pepper to taste

<u>Procedure</u>

- Set the cooker to Sauté mode and add the garlic, onion, bacon and olive oil. Make everything tender and do not burn.
- Add chicken broth, potatoes, celery, carrots, parsley, Italian seasoning and red pepper flakes. Close the lid, lock it into place, close the vent and set timer for 20 minutes.
- When time is up, allow pressure to reduce naturally
- When pressure is reduced, open the lid and remove the bacon and use it in another dish or discard.
- Add 2 more cups of broth and the evaporated milk and mix.
- With an immersion blender, process the contents till there are small chunks of potato.
- Season with salt and pepper and serve.

Chowder with Bacon and Potato

<u>Ingredients</u>

- Russet potatoes, peeled and cubed- 5 lbs.
- Sliced Celery- 3 stalks
- Diced Onion- 1 small
- Minced Garlic- 1 clove
- Seasoning Salt0- 1 tablespoon
- Ground pepper- 1 teaspoon.
- Chicken Stock- 4 cups
- Crisp bacon, chopped- 1 lb.
- Heavy Cream- 1 cup
- Whole Milk- ½ cup
- Sour Cream, Cheddar Cheese and green onion to garnish

<u>Procedure</u>

- Place all the potatoes in the inner pot of the cooker.
- Add celery, salt, onion, pepper and butter and mix well.
- To this mixture add bacon and pour the chicken broth over it.
- Close the lid, lock it into place, close the vent and set timer for 10 minutes.
- When time is up, allow pressure to reduce naturally
- When pressure is reduced, open the lidand crush the vegetables using a potato masker.
- Stir in the cream and milk.
- Garnish with sour cream, shredded cheddar and green onion and serve.

BEANS

Red Lentils and Sweet Potato

Ingredients

- Peeled and Diced Onions- 1 small
- Peeled and Chopped Sweet Potato- 1
- Red Lentils- ½ cup
- Cinnamon- ½ teaspoon
- Chipotle Chili Pepper Powder- ¼ teaspoon
- Garlic Powder- ¼ teaspoon
- Sushi Rice Vinegar- 2 tablespoons
- Yeast Flakes- 1 tablespoon
- Water- 1 ½ Cups

Procedure

- Place all the ingredients in the pressure cooker, and stir them well.
- Close the lid, lock it into place, close the vent and set timer for 6 minutes.
- When time is up, allow pressure to reduce naturally
- When pressure is reduced, open the lid and remove.
- Serve with a side of hot broccoli.

Texas Chili Trail Kidney Beans

Ingredients

- Canola Oil- 2 tablespoon
- Peeled and Chopped Onions- 1
- Ground Beef- 1 ½ pounds, turkey or chicken
- Spicy Bloody Mary Mix- 2 cups
- Diced Tomatoes- 2 cans
- Drained and rinsed kidney beans- 2 cans
- Chili powder- 4 tablespoons
- Water- 1 ½ cups

Procedure

- In the pressure cooker pot, heat some oil.
- Sauté the onions for about 5 minutes till they are light brown in color.
- Add the meat and allow it to brown. Make sure you scrape all the brown bits from the bottom.
- Add the beans, chili powder and tomatoes.
- Close the lid, lock it into place, close the vent and set timer for 10 minutes.
- When time is up, allow pressure to reduce naturally
- When pressure is reduced, open the lid and remove.
- Garnish with sour cream, cheese and green onions and serve with a side of corn chips.

Pancetta and Chicken with Lentil Cassoulet

Ingredients

- Extra virgin olive oil- 5 tablespoons
- Pancetta slices- 2 ½ inch sticks
- Diced Onion- 1
- Chicken- 1 whole
- French Green Lentils- 1 pound
- Thyme Sprigs- 4
- Chicken Broth- 1 quart
- Water- 2 quarts
- Peeled and separated Garlic cloves- one full head
- Garlic Salami- ¾ pound
- Bacon Slab- 4 ounces
- Chopped Parsley- 4 tablespoons

Procedure

- Set the pressure cooker to the heat or sauté mode, heat some olive oil.
- Sauté the onions and pancetta and cook till the fat renders.
- Now add lentils, thyme, chicken, garlic, bacon and salami
- Close the lid of the cooker and set timer for 15 minutes.
- When time is up, allow pressure to reduce naturally
- When pressure is reduced, open the lid andremove the thyme and season with salt as per your liking.
- Stir in the parsley and serve warm.

Calico Beans

<u>Ingredients</u>

- Ground Beef- 1 pound
- Chopped Onion- 1 large
- Bacon pieces- 1 pound
- Pork and Beans can- 1 large
- Butter Beans- 2 cans
- Kidney Beans- 2 cans
- Stewed Tomatoes- 3 Cups
- Corn- 1 cup
- Sugar- 1 cup
- Brown Sugar- ¾ cup
- Ketchup- ½ cup
- Cider Vinegar- 3 tablespoons
- Mustard- 1 teaspoon
- Garlic- 1 teaspoon
- Liquid Smoke- 1 tablespoon

<u>Procedure</u>

- Set the pressure cooker to heat or sauté.Cook the bacon until almost crisp. Take the drippings out and place separately.
- To the bacon, add the hamburger and onions. Pour in some of the bacon drippings.
- Close the lid, lock it into place, close the vent and set timer for 20minutes.
- When time is up, allow pressure to reduce naturally
- When pressure is reduced, open the lid and remove.
- Your dish is ready to serve.

Cassoulet in a Cooker

Ingredients

- Olive Oil- 2 tablespoons
- Boneless Pork Ribs- 2 pounds
- Great Northern Beans- 2 cups
- Beef Broth- 1 cup
- Diced Carrot- 1
- Diced Celery- 1 stalk
- Diced white onion- ½
- Dried rosemary- 2 tablespoons
- Minced Garlic- 4 cloves
- Croutons- 2 cups
- Crumbled goat Cheese- 1 cup

Procedure

- In a large skillet heat olive oil.
- Season the pork ribs with salt and pepper and brown in the olive oil
- Place the browned ribs into the pressure cooker and add beans, carrot, broth, celery, rosemary and garlic.
- Close the lid, lock it into place, close the vent and set timer for 30 minutes.
- When time is up, allow pressure to reduce naturally
- When pressure is reduced, open the lid and remove.
- Serve with a topping of croutons and goat cheese.

Beans n Chili

<u>Ingredients</u>

- Pinto Beans- 2 cups
- Chili powder- 1 tablespoon
- Cumin Seed- 1 tablespoon
- Green Chilies- 2 can
- Beef Broth- 2 cans
- Diced Tomato- 1 can
- Diced Onion- 1
- Garlic- 2 gloves
- Ground Chuck- 2 lb.
- Diced Jalapenos (Optional)

<u>Procedure</u>

- Set the pressure cooker to sauté or heat add olive oil, brown the ground chuck and let it caramelize. Add a can of diced tomatoes.
- Add the beans in to the pressure cooker. Close the lid, lock it into place, close the vent and set timer for 25 minutes. (on beans mode, if possible)
- When time is up, allow pressure to reduce naturally
  - When pressure is reduced, open the lid and remove.
- Once the cycle is complete, check the seasoning and repeat the cycle, if needed. Allow the pressure to release naturally.
- Serve with tacos.

Indian Style Chickpea Curry

Ingredients

- Dry Chickpeas- 2 cups
- Diced Onion- 1
- Diced Tomatoes- 1 can
- Choley Masala (Indian Spice) – 2 tablespoons
- Garlic Powder- 1 teaspoon
- Ginger Paste- 1 tablespoon
- Cooking Oil- 4- 6 tablespoons
- Turmeric- 1 teaspoon
- Salt to taste
- Lemon Juice- 2 -4 tablespoons
- Coriander leaves to garnish

Procedure

- Cook the chickpeas with 2 cups of water for about 15 minutes. Skim off the frothing. Strain the chickpeas and keep aside.
- In the pressure cooker heat some oil and sauté the spices.
- Heat the garam masala in the oil.
- Add the diced onions and allow them to become transparent.
- Add ginger and garlic and continue sauté
- Add the diced tomatoes and allow it to cook a bit.
- Add 2 tablespoons of choley masala.
- Close the lid, lock it into place, close the vent and set timer for 25 minutes.
- When time is up, allow pressure to reduce naturally
- When pressure is reduced, open the lid and remove.
- Garnish with lemon juice and coriander and serve with naan or chapattis.

Special Baked Beans

Ingredients

- Small white beans- 1 lb
- Diced Onion- 1 small
- Garlic- cloves
- Molasses- 1/3 cup
- Maple syrup- 1/3 cup
- Mustard Powder- 1 tablespoon
- Balsamic Vinegar- 1/8 Cup
- Ground Pepper- 4 cups
- Salt to taste

Procedure

- Transfer the beans to the cooker.
- Pour 3cups of water.
- Close the lid, lock it into place, close the vent and set timer for 10 minutes.
- When time is up, allow pressure to reduce naturally
- When pressure is reduced, open the lid and remove.
- Skim the frothing and add the rest of the ingredients. You can top up with water if needed.
- Pressure cook on 'bean' setting and allow it to cook for 15 more minutes.
- Allow the pressure to release naturally and serve with some bread.

Sweet and Spicy Beans

Ingredients

- Red Beans- 1 bag
- Chopped Yellow Onion- 1 small
- Minced Garlic- 4 cloves
- Crisp apple, peeled and chopped- 1
- Dark Brown Sugar- ¼ cup
- Ketchup- 10 tablespoons
- Sea salt- 1 tablespoon
- Celery Salt- a dash
- Cayenne Pepper- to season
- Black Pepper- 1 teaspoon
- Cumin Powder- to season

Procedure

- Place the beans and the rest of the ingredients in a pressure cooker
- Add water or broth to cover ingredients
- Close the lid, lock it into place, close the vent and set timer for 20 minutes.
- When time is up, allow pressure to reduce naturally
- When pressure is reduced, open the lid and stir and remove.
- Serve when the dish has cooled a little.

FOR THE VEGETARIANS

This section is dedicated especially to the vegetarians. It is surprising how many different types of vegetarian dishes exist across the world. So, if any of your meat eater friends told you that vegetarians have a limited choice in cuisine, call them over and surprise them!

Rice Casserole with Squash

<u>Ingredients</u>

- Oil- 2 tablespoons
- Finely Chopped Celery- 2 sticks
- Carrots, washed and chopped- 2
- Finely Chopped red pepper- 1
- Crushed Garlic- 2 cloves
- Dried Thyme- 1 tsp
- Diced White Mushrooms- 8
- Vegetable Stock- 2-3 cups
- Chopped Tomatoes- 1 tin
- Salt and Pepper to season

<u>Procedure</u>

- Set the cooker on Sauté mode. Heat the oil and cook the celery, carrots and red peppers till they are tender.
- Add the thyme, garlic, salt and pepper. Now stir the mushrooms in.
- Add some rice and mix well.
- Transfer the ingredients into a bowl that will fit into the cooker and cover with aluminum foil. Add tomatoes to the bowl to make the rice sticky.
- In the cooker add water to a height of 1 ½ inches and place the bowl in it.

- Close the lid, lock it into place, close the vent and set timer for 20 minutes.
- When time is up, allow pressure to reduce naturally
- When pressure is reduced, open the lid and remove.

Mashed Carrots

Ingredients

- Butter- 2 tablespoons
- Peeled and Cut Carrots- 1 cup
- Baking Soda- ¼ tsp

Procedure
- In the cooker, melt some butter and add the carrots and the baking soda
- Close the lid and Pressure Cook for about 4 minutes.
- Serve the delicious caramelized carrots with bread.
- This can also be done with beets.

Marinated and Seared Artichokes

Ingredients

- Artichokes- 4
- Fresh Lemon Juice- 2 tablespoons
- Balsamic Vinegar- 2 teaspoons
- Olive Oil- ½ Cup
- Dried Oregano- 1 teaspoon
- Minced Garlic- 2 cloves
- Sea Salt- ½ teaspoon
- Ground Black Pepper- ¼ teaspoon

Procedure

- Wash the artichokes well. Cut about ½ inch from the base and the top inch off. Trim the thorny tips off.
- Place the artichokes in the inner pot of the pressure cooker with about 2 cups of water. .
- Close the lid, lock it into place, close the vent and set timer for 8 minutes.
- When time is up, allow pressure to reduce naturally
- When pressure is reduced, open the lid and remove.
- Take artichokes and cut them in half. Remove the prickly leaves. Scrape the thistle fuzz off the artichoke heart.
- Prepare a marinade of lemon juice, balsamic vinegar, olive oil, oregano and salt and pepper. Shift the contents into a small jar with a lid. Shake well and set aside.
- Drizzle the marinade over the artichokes and toss them around. Coat the artichokes well and allow them to sit for 30 minutes.
- When they are ready, sear them and grill on a BBQ or grill pan for about 5 minutes.

Breakfast a la Wheat and Vegetable

Ingredients

- Wheat Berries- 2 cups
- Oil or Butter- 1 tablespoon
- Salt- 1 tablespoon
- Medium Potatoes, cubed- 2
- Carrots- 2 cups, sliced
- Sliced Onion- 1
- Celery, Sliced- 5 stalks
- Garlic Cloves- 2-4
- Poultry Seasoning- 1 teaspoon
- Thyme- 1/8 teaspoon

Procedure

- Set the cooker to the multigrain setting. Add all ingredients except onions, celery and garlic.
- Close the lid, lock it into place, close the vent and set timer for 20 minutes.
- When time is up, allow pressure to reduce naturally
- When pressure is reduced, open the lid and remove.
- Sauté the onions, celery and garlic in a separate pan.
- Add the sautéed vegetables and the seasoning to the pot and simmer for ½ an hour till the flavors mix well.
- Garnish with some parsley and serve with yoghurt

served chilled.

Kichdi Daal

Ingredients

- Lentils- 1/2 cup
- Rice- 1 cup
- Curry Leaves- 6
- Cumin Seeds- 1 teaspoon
- Ginger, crated- 1 inch stick
- Turmeric- ½ teaspoon
- Green Chilies- 2
- Salt
- Water
- Oil- 2 teaspoons

Procedure

- Set the cooker to Sauté mode and heat the oil.
- Sauté the cumin seeds, slit green chilies, the curry leaves and the ginger.
- Add some turmeric and chili powder. Let it sauté for 2 minutes.
- Add the lentils and rice with salt as required
- Add water at a 1:4 proportion i.e. 4 times the measure of the rice and lentils together.
- Close the lid, lock it into place, close the vent and set timer for 10 minutes.
- When time is up, allow pressure to reduce naturally
- When pressure is reduced, open the lid and remove.

Tip: You can also add vegetables of your choice to this kichidi.

Chipotle Rice in a Pot

<u>Ingredients</u>

- Bay Leaves- 4
- Rice- 2 cups
- Water- 1 ¾ Cup
- Canola Oil- 1 ½ tablespoon
- Juice of 1 lime
- Chopped Cilantro- ½ cup
- Salt to taste

<u>Procedure</u>
- Rinse the rice and place in the cooker.
- Add hot water and bay leaves.
- Close the lid, lock it into place, close the vent and set timer for 10 minutes.
- When time is up, allow pressure to reduce quickly
- When pressure is reduced, open the lid.
- Pour oil, lime juice and sprinkle cilantro and salt over the rice. Mix Well
- Serve with lentils or any other Indian curry

Tangy Mango Daal

Ingredients

- Coconut oil- 1 tablespoon
- Ground Cumin- 1 teaspoon
- Minced Onion- 1 Minced garlic- 4 cloves
- Minced Ginger- 1 tablespoon
- Ground Coriander- 1 teaspoon
- Cayenne Pepper- 1/8 teaspoon
- Vegetable Stock- 4 cups
- Sea Salt- 1 teaspoon
- Chana Dal- 1 cup
- Ground Turmeric- 1 teaspoon
- Peeled and Diced Mangos- 2
- Juice of ½ lime
- Chopped Cilantro- ½ cup
- 2 Mangos

Procedure

- Rinse the dal well.
- Set the pressure cooker to Sauté mode and heat the coconut oil.
- Add cumin seeds and sauté well. Add onions, ginger, garlic, cayenne and sea salt and sauté till tender.
- Add the dal and the vegetable stock with turmeric. Bring the mixture to boil.
- Add the mangoes close the lid, lock it into place, close the vent and set timer for 20 minutes.
- When time is up, allow pressure to reduce naturally
- When pressure is reduced, open the lid and remove.
- Garnish with cilantro and lime juice and serve with steamed rice.

Brown Rice Spanish Style

Ingredients

- Coconut Oil- 2 tablespoons
- Diced Yellow Onion- 1 medium
- Minced Garlic- 4 cloves
- Dried Oregano- 1 tablespoon
- Tomato Paste- 2 tablespoons
- Brown Rice- 2 cups
- Vegetable broth- 3 cups
- Sea Salt- 1 cup

Procedure

- Set the cooker to the sauté mode and heat coconut oil.
- Add onion and sauté till transparent
- Now add the garlic, oregano and tomato paste. Stir for a couple of minutes till soft.
- Add in the brown rice and let the rice caramelize a bit.
- Add the vegetable stock and sea salt. Mix well.
- Close the lid, lock it into place, close the vent and set timer for 15 minutes.
- When time is up, allow pressure to reduce naturally
- When pressure is reduced, open the lid and remove.

Raisin Butter Rice

Ingredients

- Rice- 1 cup
- Butter – 2 tablespoons
- Salt to taste
- Parsley to garnish
- Long grained white rice- 3 cups
- ¼ Salted Butter
- Raisin- ½ cup

Procedure

- Wash the rice and pour into the cooker pot with the rest of the ingredients.
- Add 2 cups of water.
- Close the lid, lock it into place, close the vent and set timer for 20 minutes.
- When time is up, allow pressure to reduce naturally
- When pressure is reduced, open the lid and remove.
- Mix the ingredients well
- Garnish with parsley and serve.

Pineapple and Cauliflower Rice

<u>Ingredients</u>

- Rice- 2 cups
- Pineapple- ½ can
- Minced Cauliflower- ½
- Oil- 2 teaspoons
- Salt to taste
- 1 cup water

<u>Procedure</u>

- Place all the ingredients in the pressure cooker pot.

Close the lid, lock it into place, close the vent and set timer for 20 minutes.

When time is up, allow pressure to reduce naturally

- When pressure is reduced, open the lid and remove.

DESSERTS

Who does not love desserts? That is the best part of any meal. If you can make instant desserts without the measuring cups and the complications of an oven, wouldn't it be great? Well, turns out that the electric pressure cooker is equipped to dish out some of the best desserts.

Who would have thought that delicious cheese cakes could be baked in an electric cooker? I was taken aback when I heard this, too, But, when I tried the recipe, I was completely blown away! Here is a list of some of the most exciting desserts that once could possibly make with the electric cooker. If you get a more ideas, go ahead and have a blast cooking with your EPC.

Lemon Cheesecake

Ingredients

For the Crust

- Graham Cracker crumbs- ½ cup
- Melted Butter- 2 tablespoons
- Sugar- 2 tablespoons

For the Cheesecake

- Cream Cheese- 16 ounces
- Sugar- 1.2 cup
- Eggs- 3
- Lemon Squeezed- 1 tablespoon
- Grated Lemon Zest- 1 teaspoon
- Vanilla Extract- ½ teaspoons
- Flour- 2 tablespoons

Process

The Crust

- Mix the butter and the sugar well.
- Mix well with the crumbs.
- Coat a pan with the crumbs and press the base in to adhere to the edges

The Cheesecake filling

- Blend the Cream Cheese and sugar till it is smooth.
- Blend in the eggs, vanilla extract, lemon zest and the lemon juice.
- Pour this batter over the crust.
- In the electric pressure cooker, pour 2 cups of water and place the trivet. The water level should not go up to the base of the trivet. Make sure you leave some gap.
- Centre the cheesecake on the trivet and place in the pressure cooker.
- Close the lid, lock it into place, close the vent and set timer for 20 minutes.
- When time is up, allow pressure to reduce naturally
- When pressure is reduced, open the lid and take the cheese cake out. If there is any additional water, blot with a tissue paper.
- Cover with plastic wrap and refrigerate for 4 hours.
- Garnish with blueberry sauce and serve.

Sweet Cheese Flan

Ingredients

- Condensed Milk- 1 can
- Evaporated milk- 1 can
- Cream cheese, softened- 1 bar
- Vanilla extract- 1 teaspoon
- Cinnamon – a dash
- Nutmeg – a dash
- Caramel
- Sugar- 6 teaspoons

Procedure

- Place the cream cheese in a medium sized bowl.
- Whisk the eggs in one at a time till they blend in fully. Add the remaining ingredients and mix.
- Coat a bowl with the caramel and pour this mixture in.
- In the cooker pot, pour some water.
- Place the caramelizedbowl on a trivet and lower into the pressure cooker.
- Close the lid, lock it into place, close the vent and set timer for 15 minutes.
- When time is up, allow pressure to reduce naturally
- When pressure is reduced, open the lid and remove.

Ginger Risotto on Pineapples

<u>Ingredients</u>

- Nondairy milk- 4 cups
- Risotto Rice- 1 ¾ cup
- Unsweetened coconut- ½ cup
- Pineapple- 1 can
- Candied Ginger- ¼ cup

<u>Procedure</u>

- Place the ingredients in the pressure cooker pot.
- Close the lid, lock it into place, close the vent and set timer for 12 minutes.
- When time is up, allow pressure to reduce naturally
- When pressure is reduced, open the lid and remove.

Coconut Rice Pudding with Mango

<u>Ingredients</u>

- Arborio Rice- ¾ cup
- Water 1 ½ cups
- Coconut Milk- 1 can
- Salt- 1 teaspoon
- Brown Sugar- 1/3 cup
- Half and Half- ½ cup
- Vanilla- 1 teaspoon
- Peeled and Cubed Mango- 1
- Shredded coconuts and broken almonds to garnish

<u>Procedure</u>

- In the pressure cooker, add the rice, coconut milk and salt.
- Close the lid, lock it into place, close the vent and set timer for 10 minutes.
- When time is up, allow pressure to reduce naturally
- When pressure is reduced, open the lid and remove.
- Add the chopped mango, half and half and vanilla and stir well.
- Top with coconut and almond and serve in small bowls.

Special Rice Pudding

Ingredients

- Whole grain black sticky rice- 2 cups
- Coconut Milk- 1 can
- Sugar- ½ cup
- Salt- ½ teaspoon
- Sesame seeds, roasted- 2 tablespoons
- Shredded coconut, sliced strawberries and mint leaves to garnish

Procedure

- Wash and Drain the rice well and place in a large bowl that can fit into the pressure cooker. Add some boiling water just to cover the rice. Place the bowl on a trivet and lower in the pressure cooker with 2-3 inches of water.
- Close the lid, lock it into place, close the vent and set timer for 30 minutes.
- When time is up, allow pressure to reduce naturally
- When pressure is reduced, open the lid and remove.
- Meanwhile, make the coconut sauce by heating sugar, salt and coconut water in a sauce pan.
- Once the rice is done, add ½ the sauce to coat the rice fully. Make sure it is not to watery. Allow the mixture to stand for 20 minutes.
- Serve the rice with a topping of the remaining sauce, strawberries, coconut and mint leaves.

Apple Butter

Ingredients

- Apples- 1 peck
- Cinnamon- 1 teaspoon
- Sugar- As per taste
- Nutmeg- a dash

Procedure

- Line the inner pot of the cooker with the apples.
- Add 1 cup of water.
- Close the lid, lock it into place, close the vent and set timer for 5minutes.
- When time is up, allow pressure to reduce naturally
- When pressure is reduced, open the lid and remove. Cut the apples into pieces
- With an immersion blender, blend the apple till it reaches the consistency of apple butter.
- Add the seasoning and sugar and mix well.
- Store in canning jars and leave them in a water bath.
- Serve with waffles and baked bread.

Bread Pudding in Steam

<u>Ingredients</u>

- Coconut Oil- 1 teaspoon
- Coconut Milk- 1 can
- Whole Milk- 1 cup
- Beaten eggs- 3
- Staled Bread, cubed- 4 cups
- Cran-raisins- ½ cup
- Cinnamon- 1 teaspoon
- Salt- a pinch
- Vanilla- ½ teaspoon
- Nuts of your choice to garnish

<u>Procedure</u>

- Add 2 cups of water to the pressure cooker. Place the steam rack in the water.
- In a small casserole, add the bread, coconut milk and whole milk.
- Mix in the rest of the ingredients and cover the casserole with wax paper
- Place on the rack.
- Close the lid, lock it into place, close the vent and set timer for 10 minutes.
- When time is up, allow pressure to reduce naturally
- When pressure is reduced, open the lid and remove.
- Broil the pudding to get a brown crust.
- Serve with a topping of your favorite nuts.

Bread in a Coffee Can

Ingredients

- Bread Mix of your choice
- Oil or butter to grease the can
- Flour- 2 tablespoons

Procedure

- Mix up the instant bread mix.
- Grease a coffee can with butter and flour the insides.
- Roll the bread mix into a soft ball and place inside the can
- Cover the can with foil and place in a cooker with 8 cups of water.
- Close the lid, lock it into place, close the vent and set timer for 15 minutes.
- When time is up, allow pressure to reduce naturally
- When pressure is reduced, open the lid and slide the bread out.
- Let it cool and Serve

Steamed and Sweetened Eddoes

<u>Ingredients</u>

- Eddoes- 2 pounds
- White Sugar/Maple Syrup/Brown Sugar

<u>Procedure</u>

- Wash the eddoes thoroughly.
- Place a steaming rack in the pressure cooker and pour 2 cups of water around it.
- Place the eddoes in a ceramic bowl and place in the rack.
- Close the lid, lock it into place, close the vent and set timer for 8 minutes.
- When time is up, allow pressure to reduce naturally
- When pressure is reduced, open the lid and remove.
- Peel of the shell of the eddoes and roll in maple syrup, white sugar or brown sugar and serve.

Red Bean Soup

<u>Ingredients</u>

- Red Beans- 2 cups
- Dry Lotus Seeds- 1.2 cup
- Dry Chestnuts- ½ cup
- Dried Mandarin- 2 pieces
- Sugar- 4 tablespoons
- Water- 8 to 10 cups

<u>Procedure</u>

- Place all the ingredients in the cooker.
- Close the lid, lock it into place, close the vent and set timer for 20 minutes. (on benas mode, if possible)
- When time is up, allow pressure to reduce naturally
- When pressure is reduced, open the lid and remove.
- Open the lid, stir well and serve.

BONUS RECIPES

Ok, here are some of my personal favorites that I have added as a bonus. These are comfort foods that you can enjoy at any time of the year

Turkey Breast in Gravy

<u>Ingredients</u>

- Frozen Turkey Breast with Gravy Packet- 1
- Whole Onion-1

<u>Procedure</u>

- Wash the frozen turkey and remove the plastic. Retain the net.
- In the pressure cooker, place the turkey with the whole onion and the gravy packet.
- Close the lid, lock it into place, close the vent and set timer for 30 minutes.
- When time is up, allow pressure to reduce naturally
- When pressure is reduced, open the lid and remove the mesh, slice the turkey and serve.

Osso Bucco

Ingredients

- Veal or lamb shanks, diced- 4
- Flour- 1/4 cup
- Black Pepper- ½ teaspoon
- Salt to taste
- Garlic Powder- ½ teaspoon
- Onion Powder- ½ teaspoon
- Thyme- 1 teaspoon
- Olive Oil- ¼ cup
- Rosemary- 1 teaspoon
- Butter- 1 tablespoon
- Carrots, diced- 2
- Chopped Onion – 1
- Crushed Garlic- 2 cloves
- Chicken Broth- 3 cups
- Red Potatoes- 2 lbs.
- Butter- 2 tablespoons

Procedure

- In a large bowl, add the seasonings and the flour.
- Blend together. Roll the shanks in the flour mix and set aside
- Preheat a large skillet and add the oil and bring it to smoke.
- Place the shanks in the oil and brown all sides.
- Set them aside when they are done.
- To the remaining oil, add flour to make the rue
- Loosen the rue with the broth and make a sauce
- Pour the sauce into the pressure cooker and place the shanks in the sauce.
- Place chopped vegetables in the gaps and pour the remaining sauce over.
- Close the lid, lock it into place, close the vent and set timer for40 minutes.

- When the cooking cycle is almost done, boil and mash the red potatoes with butter. Season with salt and pepper
- When time is up, allow pressure to reduce naturally
- When pressure is reduced, open the lid and remove.

.

- Serve the lamb shanks on a bed of potatoes.

Potato and Fish cooked in Beer

Ingredients

- Fish Fillet – 1 pound
- Peeled and Diced potatoes- 4
- Beer- 1 cup
- Red Pepper Sliced- 1
- Oil- 1 tablespoon
- Oyster Sauce- 1 tablespoon
- Rock Candy- 1 tablespoon
- Salt to taste

Procedure

- Place all the ingredients in the pressure cooker. Place fish fillet on top of veggies.
- Close the lid, lock it into place, close the vent and set timer for 15minutes.
- When time is up, allow pressure to reduce naturally
- When pressure is reduced, open the lid and carefully remove the fish, it will be very soft.

Congee

Ingredients

- Sticky Rice- 1/4 cup
- Brown rice- ¼ cup
- Peanut- 1/8 cup
- Red Bean- 1/8 cup
- Minced Walnut- 1/8 cup
- Sesame- 1/8 cup
- Minced Chestnut- 1/8 cup
- Red Date- 1/8 cup
- Rock Candy- ½ cup
- Water- 3 cups

Procedure

- Place all the ingredients in the pressure cooker.
- Close the lid, lock it into place, close the vent and set timer for 30 minutes.
- When time is up, allow pressure to reduce naturally
- When pressure is reduced, open the lid and remove.

The best thing about all the cooker recipes is that the nutrition is retained completely. They are fast, delicious and simple. There are a few secrets to convert your favorite recipe into an electric pressure cooker recipe. I have discussed this in the final chapter.

Custard in a Jiffy

<u>Ingredients</u>

- Milk- 2 cups
- Eggs-2
- Sugar-1/3 cup
- Vanilla-1/2 teaspoon
- Water

<u>Procedure</u>

- Heat the milk and let it cook
- Stir in the eggs and sugar, mixing constantly.
- Add vanilla extract.
- Place in custard cups and cover with aluminum foil.
- Place on trivet and lower in pressure cooker with water.
- Close the lid, lock it into place, close the vent and set timer for 15 minutes.
- When time is up, allow pressure to reduce naturally
- When pressure is reduced, open the lid and remove.
- Refrigerate the custard and serve

Pressure Cooking Wrapped in Foil

. You can make packets of all in one meals very fast and easy. The best results are with chicken breasts preferably boneless, skinless and split.

You can also do the same thing with fish filets.

Check out the recipes and then you will soon be creating your own.

Easy Chicken

<u>Ingredients</u>

- 4 chicken breasts with bone
- Italian dressing
- Salt, pepper
- 4 slices tomatoes
- Garlic powder
- 4 pats of butter
- Lemon juice
- 4 sheets of aluminum foil
- Shredded cheddar cheese

<u>Procedure</u>

Place 1 chicken breast on foil. Top with dressing, a slice of tomato, pat of butter, garlic powder, lemon juice, salt, pepper and shredded cheese. Wrap. Repeat for additional pieces.

Add trivet to the pressure cooker and add 2 cups of water. Place packets on the trivet and close and lock the lid. Set timer for 10 minutes and use the quick pressure release when done. Remove, cut open packets and transfer packets to plates.

Chicken Breast Steamed in foil with Herbs and Spinach

<u>Ingredients</u>

- 1 skinless, boneless chicken breast
- 2 sprigs fresh dill
- 1 whole scallion
- 2 tomato slices
- 4 spinach leaves, washed
- Pepper to taste
- Aluminum foil
- Olive Oil

<u>Procedure</u>

Set pressure cooker to heat or sauté. Add oil and quickly brown chicken breast on both sides. Prepare a square of foil large enough to hold the chicken. Place chicken in foil, top with dill, scallions, tomato and spinach. Add a dash of pepper. Fold over to form a neat package. Seal edges tightly.

Place trivet or rack in pressure cooker and add 1 cup of water. Place packet on trivet. Close the lid and set the timer for 8 minutes. Release pressure manually, remove packet, open and transfer to plate.

Garlic Lemon Chicken Breast

Ingredients

- 2 tablespoons grated lemon rind (fresh)
- 4-5 cloves garlic, crushed
- 2 tablespoons soy sauce
- 1/2 cup fresh lemon juice
- 2 teaspoons Hungarian paprika
- 4 boneless, skinless chicken breasts
- Olive oil
- salt, pepper, garlic powder (for sprinkling)
- 4 sprigs Italian parsley
- 4 onion slices (sliced in thick rings)
- heavy duty aluminum foil

Procedure

Cut 4 rectangles of heavy duty aluminum foil, each about the size of 1/2 a standard cookie sheet.

Combine first 5 ingredients in a blender.

Spray the 4 large rectangles of aluminum foil with olive oil. Place chicken in center; brush with the blended lemon/garlic mixture, then sprinkle with salt, pepper, and lightly dust with garlic powder. Add a tablespoon of blended mixture I center of breast.

Place a slice of onion and a sprig of parsley over each. Fold up aluminum into a loose, square packet and crimp edges tightly to seal well.

Place a trivet in the pressure cooker, add 1 1/2 cups of water and place the packets on the trivet. Set timer for 8 minutes then release pressure manually.

Barbequed Chicken Breasts

<u>Ingredients</u>

- 6-8 chicken breasts

SAUCE:

Use your favorite BBQ Sauce or if you want to make your own:

- 2 tbsp. butter
- 2 tbsp. ketchup
- 2 tbsp. lemon juice
- 4 tbsp. water
- 3 tbsp. brown sugar2 tbsp.
- Vinegar
- 5 cloves garlic, minced
- 2 tbsp. Worcestershire sauce
- 2 tsp. dry mustard
- 2 tsp. paprika
- 2 tsp. salt
- 2 tsp. chili powder
- 1/2 tsp. red pepper

<u>Procedure</u>

Remove skin from chicken breasts or use skinless breasts. Place each one in a piece of heavy duty aluminum foil that has been sprayed with olive oil. Cup foil around chicken so it will hold the sauce and pour sauce over each piece. Wrap the foil tightly and seal the edges well. Combine all of the above sauce ingredients and mix well or use a blender or food processor. This will be enough to use with 6-8 chicken breasts.

Place trivet in pressure cooker and add 2 cups of water. Close the lid, seal and set timer for 12 minutes. Release pressure manually, remove packets, let cool before opening and transfer to plate.

Chicken Italian in Foil

<u>Ingredients</u>

- Italian dressing
- 2 chicken breasts
- 1/4 tsp. salt
- 1 med. potato, pared
- 1 med. Zucchini
- 2 tbsp. ketchup
- 1/2 tsp. oregano leaves
- 1 tbsp. butter

<u>Procedure</u>

Brush dressing on chicken. Sprinkle with salt. Cut zucchini into slices. Place on potato and salt. Place chicken pieces on zucchini; top with ketchup, oregano and butter. Wrap tightly in foil.

Place trivet in pressure cooker, add 1 cup of water and lock lid. Set timer for 8 minutes and then release pressure manually. Transfer to plate, cut open foil and remove contents to plate,

Fast Boiled Fish

<u>Ingredients</u>

- 4 fresh or frozen fish (any choice) fillets
- 1/2 c. bottled buttermilk salad dressing
- 2 c. broccoli flowerets
- 1 red or green pepper, cut into strips
- 1 sm. sweet onion, thinly sliced
- 1 c. fresh mushrooms, sliced

<u>Procedure</u>

Place individual fish fillets on four 12 inch pieces of foil. Spoon 2 tablespoons of dressing over each fillet. Surround each fillet with 1/4 of each vegetable. Seal each packet by rolling edges together. Set packets on trivet in pressure cooker with 2 cups of water. Close and seal lid and set timer for 5 minutes (8 minutes if frozen). Release pressure manually. Remove and serve.

Chapter 8: Conclusion

We are sure that your electric pressure cooker will be out of the attic and on your cooker counter by now. After all, the benefits of the electric pressure cooker are so many. The recipes mentioned in the previous chapter must have also helped you realize how versatile the electric pressure cooker is. From soups to desserts, you can make it all with just one vessel.

Here are a few tricks that will help you experiment with your pressure cooker. You can take any old family recipe and turn it into an easy electric pressure cooker recipe. Here are a few simple tips to help you:

- Reduce the liquid quantity by half. Conventional vessels use more liquid than the EPC as the liquids do not evaporate in the electric pressure cooker.
- If there are any foods that foam when you pressure cook, try to eliminate them. If you cannot, make sure you leave enough space on the top to let the liquid foam
- The pressure in the electric cookers varies. Use the tips given in the previous chapters to make amends with the cooking time. Usually the cooking time should be reduced by 1/3rd

This is everything that you need to know about your electric pressure cooker. We wish you many happy cooking moments that are totally stress free and easy.

Made in the USA
Middletown, DE
04 March 2015